SOCIAL INEQUALITY IN CANADA

SOCIAL INEQUALITY IN CANADA

Edited by

Alan Frizzell
Jon H. Pammett

CARLETON UNIVERSITY PRESS

Canadian Cataloguing in Publication Data

Main entry under title:

Social inequality in Canada

Includes bibliographical references.
ISBN 0-88629-279-4

1. Equality—Canada. 2. Canada—Social conditions
—1971- 3. Equality. I. Frizzell, Alan, 1947-
II. Pammett, Jon H., 1944-

HN110.Z9S6 1996   305'.0971   C96-900311-0

Cover Design: Your Aunt Nellie
Typeset: Mayhew & Associates Graphic Communications, Richmond, Ont.

Carleton University Press gratefully acknowledges the support extended to its publishing program by the Canada Council and the financial assistance of the Ontario Arts Council. The Press would also like to thank the Department of Canadian Heritage, Government of Canada, and the Government of Ontario through the Ministry of Culture, Tourism and Recreation, for their assistance.

TABLE OF CONTENTS

LIST OF TABLES

CHAPTER ONE

THE ISSP AND INTERNATIONAL RESEARCH
AN INTRODUCTION

Alan Frizzell

IT IS HARDLY SURPRISING that most social science research in Canada is concerned with matters central to the Canadian experience. Questions of national unity, national identity, and political, economic, and social attempts to deal with problems of geography, language, and the ethnic mix have provided fertile ground for academic research. All of this is understandable, but there is a case to be made that a full analysis of what any country "is" and what its values and goals "are" must incorporate a comparative perspective. There is much debate in Canada as to how Canadians differ from or resemble citizens of other countries, particularly the United States. Is it true that Canadians are more tolerant and deferential than their southern neighbours, or that they are more environmentally friendly than most Europeans, or that they are more accepting of immigration than just about any other Western country? It is through comparisons such as these that a true picture of national identity emerges.

To facilitate comparative research there is a plethora of international statistics. Aggregate data can do much to show differences and similarities between nations. Census and other data can paint a statistical portrait of a country in terms of birth rates, years spent in education, production levels, budget allocations, and so on. These are invaluable indicators of a nation's social, economic, and political priorities. Another form of comparison is to examine institutions in several countries. Most of the earliest forms of comparative research are of this type. Differences in political, social, bureaucratic, or military systems again provide information about national imperatives.

But does all of this explain how Canadians differ from the British, the Swedes, or the Turks? Clearly the data provide glimpses of an answer to the question, but it would be much more satisfying to probe national attitudes on a variety of social and political issues in order to discover how a national experience has shaped a national identity and national priorities. If that could be done in a co-ordinated way in several countries, then the value of comparative research would be much enhanced and the attendant difficulties much reduced.

Since there is already a considerable literature on Canadian identity and values, why bother with comparative research? The reason is that the debate on identity would be enriched. According to Ramsay Cook, Canadian identity tends to be composed of residual elements of U.S. and British culture, and while we can identify specific factors, such as Northern Toryism, multiculturalism, and bilingualism as elements of a Canadian culture, the nation suffers from a kind of Portnoy's complaint because of a "failure to develop a secure and unique identity" (Cook, 1977, 185). On the other hand, Seymour Martin Lipset says that "Canada ... lacks an ideology, but it has a strong identity, one that is reflected in its increasingly important literature and other creative arts" (Lipset, 1990, 57). These are mere examples of the kind of analyses that abound in Canada: on the one hand a lament that Canadians have failed miserably to develop unique national symbols that would somehow represent their essence, and on the other an assumption that achievements, whether in the arts, sports, or the economy, magically represent the national will or spirit.

Analyses that do not deal with Canadian attitudes and values present a rather limited view of national identity. For attitudes are important. Ever since Weber defined power as the ability to achieve goals even in the face of resistance, social theorists have been interested in the notion of power not based solely on force or structural factors. The achievement of a legitimating "mandate" ensuring acquiescence requires an appropriate attitudinal framework (Giddens, 1977). This, however, should not be confused with nationalism or national identity. As recent events in Eastern Europe have shown, myopic nationalism can serve to limit attitudinal scope.

For most societies attitudinal frameworks must be complex and comprehensive. In fact, a society can be defined as "a complex structure of logically linked belief variables shared by most of a group's members, about what motivates people; how the group is organized; who should get what, when and how; what roles each person is allowed or forced to assume; and how, overall, the group is to be organized" (Lane, 1994, 364-65). Inglehart (1977, 1985) argues that attitudinal studies are ever more important since generational change rates have increased and, more important, for many societies primary material needs have been met, and that the value priority in mass publics is related to a postmaterial environment. Whether or not one accepts the Inglehart position on postmaterialism, the subject of the attitudinal and value structure of society is an important one.

Why then has so little cross-national attitudinal research been done by Canadian researchers? Firstly, there is an understandable focus on the manifest social and political problems in a society beset with profound and deep cleavages. In four recent years of the *Canadian Journal of Political Science*, only four articles of a comparative nature could be discovered. These dealt with diplomacy (Cooper, 1992), protectionist legislation (Jenson, 1989), press coverage (Soderlund, 1990), and super-power crises (James & Harvey, 1989); only two included Canada in the analysis. More attitudinal research and more comparative research on values and attitudes would help put Canadian problems in perspective. Canada is not the only country in the world with linguistic, geographical, and ethnic/cultural cleavages! In addition, in an era of internationalism it is important to know how the Canadian community relates to other communities with which it has to deal.

Existing comparative research has tended to be limited to institutions or sectors. While it can be useful to compare institutions, the conclusions one can draw are limited, since the exercise is one of configurative description and suffers from a surfeit of formal-legalism (an example is Fry, 1984). It is also dangerous to assume, as Blondel (1973) does, that structures are a function of values and attitudes, especially in those countries where political and social structures are legacies from the past and where reform of those very structures has proved difficult.

Studies of social behaviour encounter problems when national boundaries are crossed. In political science, the early work on voting patterns in the United States has been copied in many countries. While many of the measures used in American analyses have proved useful in other countries, one major early conclusion, that the primary predictor of vote was *party identification*, a psychological identification which can persist without legal recognition or evidence of formal "membership or even without a consistent record of party support" (Campbell, Converse, Miller, Stokes, 1960, 21), has proven to be less than useful when applied to many other countries, including Canada (Clarke, Jenson, LeDuc, & Pammett, 1979). Thus while institutional description and behavioural analysis are insightful, they are incomplete in themselves.

Even when cross-national attitudinal research is done, there are problems of significance and meaning. In one of the earliest and most compelling analyses of comparative political systems that used attitudinal data, Almond and Verba (1963) claimed to identify the "civic culture," one that combined modernity with tradition, that exhibited high levels of political efficacy and trust, and that maintained a judicious mixture of respect for authority along with a sturdy independence, as the ideal political culture to ensure a stable, democratic state. Though this model led to a new era of comparative political research, the theoretical framework developed by Almond and Verba has had numerous limitations. Over time, many states that do not possess some of the fundamental prerequisites of a civic culture have proved remarkably stable and durable. So, does Canada have a civic culture (or an Anglo-American political system), or does it constitute a consociational democracy, where diversity of interest leads to group accommodation (Lijphart, 1969)? The answer may well be that general political descriptions of this type are to be used with caution. It is as hard to define the essence of a political culture as it is to define the average citizen, the man on the Clapham omnibus in England or Monsieur Tout le Monde in France. Although any researcher "would like to be able to identify quickly the regularities and differences between systems and to come up with a simple explanation for them ... rarely, if ever, can this be achieved in practice" (Macridis & Ward, 1963, 5).

Does this then mean that attempts at comparative attitudinal research are to be abandoned or focused on specific and narrowly defined topics? Of course it does not, but it does mean that general theories and grand conclusions should be avoided, and, like Wittgenstein's propositions in the Tractatus, the findings of international attitudinal research should be used as "ladders to understanding." If one accepts that, then the question becomes how best to proceed? The technical problems of doing comparative attitudinal research are fairly obvious. Rokkan (1968) and his colleagues identified many years ago the problems of defective classification, multicausality, pluricausality, intervening variables, coincidence, personal factors, translation, and equivalence of indices as some of the most important. But with planning and understanding, many technical problems can be solved. More serious are the problems of organizing and funding large-scale, co-ordinated, cross-national research over time. It was an attempt to solve this problem that led to the creation of the International Social Survey Programme.

WHAT IS THE ISSP?

Many differences exist between nations, and the consequences of those differences can range from economic and social communion to war. How best to study them using the techniques of social science? In 1980 four research teams, from Great Britain, the United States, West Germany, and Australia, decided to add a module of collectively designed common questions to existing national social surveys. These were the British Social Attitudes Survey, the American General Social Survey, the German ALLBUS, and the Australian National Social Science Survey. The researchers recognized that "public attitudes are as much a part of social reality as are behaviour patterns, social conditions or demographic characteristics. Some social attitudes are also no less slow to change. Yet their rigorous measurement, particularly across nations, has never been accorded a very high priority. The ISSP is, we hope, helping to rectify this omission" (Davis & Jowell, 1989, 11). A Nuffield Foundation grant allowed the four groups to hold meetings to further international collaboration between the existing surveys, which led to the formation of the ISSP. The founding members agreed 1) to jointly develop survey modules dealing with important areas of social science; 2) to field the modules as fifteen-minute supplements to the regular national surveys (or as a special survey as necessary); 3) to include an extensive common core of background variables; and 4) to make the data available to the wider social science community as soon as possible.

The notion that survey analysis can surmount language, cultural, system, and demographic boundaries requires care with question design and translation, extensive consultation on variables used, and, most important, a common methodology. In addition, the data sets have to be combined, stored in, and distributed from a central location. Thanks to the Zentralarchiv für Empirische Sozialforshchung at the University of Cologne this last condition was met.

Since 1983 the ISSP has grown to include 25 nations: the founding four—Australia, Germany, Great Britain, and the United States—plus

Austria, Bulgaria, Canada, the Czech Republic, Hungary, Ireland, Israel, Italy, Japan, the Netherlands, New Zealand, Norway, the Philippines, Poland, Russia, Slovenia, Spain, and Sweden. Cyprus, Finland, and France will field their first surveys in 1996. Each year committees of the member nations are appointed to develop designated topics into questionnaire form and these are presented to the full annual plenary. Such topics include "Social Inequality," the "Environment," "Issues affecting Women," "Role of Government," and "National Identity." Modules on these topics are repeated at regular intervals to provide tracking data.

The ISSP marks several new departures in cross-national research. First, the collaboration between organizations is not ad hoc or intermittent, but routine and continual. Second, while necessarily more circumscribed than collaboration dedicated solely to cross-national research on a single topic, the ISSP makes cross-national research a basic part of the research agenda of each participating country. Third, by combining a cross-time with a cross-national perspective, two powerful research designs are being used together to study societal processes.

The Carleton University Survey Centre was chosen to represent Canada in the ISSP after competition in 1991. The objective of the surveys that have subsequently been carried out in this country is to measure the consistency and logic of social attitudes in Canada and to compare these to those of 24 other countries. Each Canadian survey complies with the ISSP methodology standards in using a multi-stage random sample (stratified by province), a self-completion format, and a sample size of over one thousand. The data are processed at Carleton University and sent to the archive in Cologne. The data from the Canadian module is made available through the Carleton University Library Data Archive, as is the combined ISSP data set when compiled by the Zentralarchiv.

REFERENCES

Almond, Gabriel, & Sidney Verba. (1963). *The Civic Culture.* Princeton: Princeton University Press.

Blondel, Jean. (1973). *Comparing Political Systems.* London: Weidenfeld and Nicholson.

Campbell, Angus, Philip Converse, Warren Miller, & Donald Stokes. (1960) *The American Voter.* New York: John Wiley.

Clarke, Harold, Jane Jenson, Lawrence LeDuc, & Jon H. Pammett. (1979). *Political Choice in Canada.* Toronto: McGraw-Hill Ryerson.

Cook, Ramsay. (1977). *The Maple Leaf Forever: Essays on Nationalism and Politics in Canada.* Toronto: Macmillan.

Cooper, Andrew. (1992). Like-Minded Nations and Contrasting Diplomatic Styles: Australian and Canadian Approaches to Agricultural Trade. *Canadian Journal of Political Science, 25,* 349-80.

Davis, James A., & Roger Jowell. (1989). Measuring Social Differences: An Introduction to the International Social Survey Programme. In Roger Jowell, Sharon Witherspoon, Lindsay Brook Eds., *British Social Attitudes: Special International Report,* (pp. 1-13) London: Gower.

Fry, Earl H. (1984). *Canadian Government and Politics in Comparative Perspective.* Lanham MD: University Press of America.

Giddens, Antony. (1977). *Studies in Social and Political Theory.* London: Hutchison.

Inglehart, Ronald. (1977). *The Silent Revolution.* Princeton: Princeton University Press. (1985).

———— New Perspectives on Value Change. *Comparative Political Studies, 17,* 485-532.

James, Patrick, & Frank Harvey. (1989). Threat Escalation and Crisis Stability: Superpower Cases 1948-1979. *Canadian Journal of Political Science, 22,* 523-46.

Jenson, Jane. (1989). Paradigms and Political Discourse: Protective Legislation in France and the United States Before 1914. *Canadian Journal of Political Science, 22,* 235-58.

Lane, Ruth. (1994). Political Culture: Residual Category or General Theory. *Comparative Political Studies, 25,* 362-87.

Lijphart, Arend. (1969). Consociational Democracy. *World Politics, 21,* 207-25.

Lipset, Seymour Martin. (1990). *Continental Divide: The Values and Institutions of the United States and Canada.* New York: Routledge.

Macridis, Roy, & Robert Ward (Eds.). (1963). *Modern Political Systems: Europe.* Englewood Cliffs NJ: Prentice-Hall.

Rokkan, Stein (Ed.). (1968). *Comparative Research Across Cultures and Nations.* Paris: Mouton.

Soderlund, Walter. (1990). A Comparison of Press Coverage in Canada and the U.S. of the 1982 and 1984 Salvodoran Elections. *Canadian Journal of Political Science, 23,* 59-72.

CHAPTER TWO

INDICATORS OF SOCIAL INEQUALITY IN CANADA
WOMEN, ABORIGINAL PEOPLES,
AND VISIBLE MINORITIES

Jeffrey Frank

THE CONCEPT OF EQUALITY is difficult to define, much less to operationalize and quantify. One solution to this problem is to examine equality in terms of socio-economic status. Defined in this way, equality and the extent to which it is enjoyed by individuals or groups in society can be measured using indicators such as education, employment and income. Some would argue that such a comparison would be unfair— that the level of achievement in these areas is less important than the degree to which *equality of opportunity* is enjoyed by these individuals or groups, and, further, that responsibility for "getting ahead" in these areas rests with the individual.

This, however, is a culturally and ideologically loaded proposition. Surely the ability or even the desire to "succeed" in terms of educational attainment, occupational status, income and, ultimately, material accumulation assumes a certain set of values. Other things in life matter just as much: the quality of relationships between family, friends, and community, the extent to which daily activities are meaningful and fulfilling, and the level of one's physical, mental, and spiritual health. Of course, choosing these things as important in defining notions of equality reflects other value sets. In addition, these qualitative factors are extremely difficult to measure.

Therefore, the choice of measuring social equality in terms of education, employment, and income is made out of expediency, practicality and, to a large extent, consistency with the prevailing culture and ideology. Even after accepting that equality must be narrowly defined and operationalized in this way, one must recognize that such a definition does not begin to capture all the nuances of what most would agree the notion of equality entails. Beyond education, employment and income, equality extends to people's interactions with each other and with various institutions—interactions that involve a complex mixture of attitudes and mutual reactions. But again, if one were to attempt to capture this complexity, serious conceptual difficulties and measurement problems would arise. Therefore, little choice remains but to accept an imperfect proxy for equality, such as socio-economic status.

Despite the official recognition of different groups in the *Charter of Rights and Freedoms* and in various pieces of legislation, and even with programs designed to eliminate existing disparities, inequality persists in Canada. Certain groups in Canadian society are definitely better off than others, according to the aforementioned indicators. Some might argue that equality of opportunity exists and that this is enough: it is not the role of the state to ensure equality at all levels, but to remove barriers to equality. Even as society moves toward the removal of all such barriers, it appears that *structural inequality* remains. The purpose of this paper is not to explain why this is so, but to describe the extent to which differences in socio-economic status exist among particular groups. Using official data sources such as the Census of Canada, this paper undertakes to examine the disparities that exist for women, aboriginal peoples and visible minorities in terms of educational attainment, employment status and income.

EDUCATIONAL ATTAINMENT

Education is closely linked with labour force activity, employment, occupation and ultimately income. As formal education is normally acquired relatively early in life, and because it usually precedes achievement in other areas, it is introduced first. For purposes of clarity, educational attainment has been categorized into four levels: "Less than Grade 9," "Grades 9 to 13" (or secondary schooling), "Some postsecondary" (including community colleges, CEGEPs and other non-university institutions), and "University degree."

The Canadian population is more educated today than at any other point in history. In 1991, 11.4% of the population aged 15 and over

(2.4 million people) held a university degree, compared with 4.8% in 1971. Also in 1991, 31.7% (6.8 million) had some postsecondary education, 42.6% had Grades 9 to 13, and 14.3% had less than a Grade 9 education. In comparison, 32.3% had less than Grade 9 in 1971.

Educational attainment varies considerably across the population. This indicator is less useful in comparing different age groups. Because Canada's population has become more educated over time, it is difficult to compare seniors, for example, with the population aged 35 to 44 without taking into account this "education inflation." For this reason it is more appropriate to look at educational attainment when making comparisons between men and women or between ethnic groups. Even here, varying age structures between these groups explain some of the differences in educational attainment observed. This must be considered when making such comparisons.

EMPLOYMENT

Several concepts are useful in examining employment characteristics of various groups. The first is that of *labour force participation*. For a person to be in the labour force does not necessarily mean that he or she is employed. It simply means that a person is either working or is actively looking for work. Thus, the labour force includes the unemployed who are seeking work but excludes others, such as children under 15, retired people, and discouraged former workers. The concepts of *employment* and *unemployment* relate only to labour force participants. The employment rate is the proportion of the labour force that is working, while the unemployment rate is the proportion not working. These measures must be interpreted with care, in that an increase in the unemployment rate can signal an influx of labour force participants (people who were previously not in the labour force but who are now looking for work) or job losses among those who were previously employed. Similar care must be taken in interpreting differences in employment and unemployment between groups.

Since the mid-1960s, unemployment rates have exhibited an upward trend, with variations coinciding with periods of economic expansion and recession. In 1994, the average rate of unemployment across Canada remained above 10%, despite the fact that the economy was officially in a period of recovery. The average duration of unemployment episodes has also increased in recent years, more than doubling between 1975

(12 weeks) and 1993 (25 weeks). Competition for jobs is greater today than it was in the past, and this competition has the potential to exacerbate inequalities between different groups.

Even for those who are employed, the distinction between *part-time* and *full-time* work is important. Many people choose to work part-time, because of the flexibility that this type of work can afford. Others would prefer to work full-time, but have part-time work because this is all they can find. A greater proportion of the labour force works part-time today (17% in 1994) than was the case at any time in the past (11% in 1976, for example).

For employed people, one can also analyze *occupation*. Any ranking of occupations in terms of status or importance is arbitrary and implies certain value judgments. It is difficult to say, for example, that a professional (such as a lawyer) is more important to society than a tradesperson (such as a carpenter). Nonetheless, some sort of ordinal ranking of occupational groups must be undertaken to make comparisons between groups useful. To some extent, such a ranking implicitly takes into account other factors that are being examined separately, such as education and income.

The occupational categories used in this paper are based on Statistics Canada's 1980 Standard Occupational Classification. For the purposes of this analysis, certain normative assumptions have been made. Managerial, administrative, and related occupations, for example, have been deemed to be of higher socio-economic status than clerical, sales, and service occupations. Jobs that could be roughly categorized as *professional* include managerial, administrative, and related occupations; occupations in natural sciences, engineering, and mathematics; occupations in social sciences and related fields; teaching and related occupations; occupations in medicine and health; and artistic, literary, recreational and related occupations. *Non-professional* occupations could include clerical, sales and service occupations; various occupations found in agriculture, primary industries and manufacturing; and occupations in construction and trades. In 1991, about 30% of Canada's labour force had professional jobs, using the above distinctions.

The distribution of different groups across these occupational categories indicates that the so-called "good jobs"—those that have high educational requirements and that generally pay well—are more often held by men, although the situation is changing. Shifts in women's employment are discussed in the "Women in Canada" section later in this chapter. The table below summarizes the occupational distribution of Canada's labour force as it was at the time of the 1991 Census.

TABLE 1: EXPERIENCED LABOUR FORCE
BY OCCUPATIONAL GROUP, 1991

	Total		Men		Women	
Experienced labour force	14,220,235	100.0%	7,839,245	100.0%	6,380,985	100.0%
Managerial, administrative	1,739,165	12.2%	1,086,150	13.9%	653,015	10.2%
Natural sciences, engineering	572,515	4.0%	458,325	5.8%	114,190	1.8%
Social sciences	316,365	2.2%	122,650	1.6%	193,715	3.0%
Teaching	626,520	4.4%	224,730	2.9%	401,790	6.3%
Medicine and health	727,335	5.1%	151,490	1.9%	575,845	9.0%
Religion, artistic, literary	279,195	2.0%	162,665	2.1%	116,535	1.8%
Clerical	2,573,060	18.1%	556,395	7.1%	2,016,665	31.6%
Sales	1,308,705	9.2%	707,085	9.0%	601,625	9.4%
Services	1,818,375	12.9%	795,030	10.1%	1,023,345	16.0%
Farming, horticulture	474,360	3.3%	342,310	4.4%	132,050	2.1%
Fishing, trapping, forestry, mining	195,955	1.4%	180,890	2.3%	15,060	0.2%
Processing	410,665	2.9%	304,495	3.9%	106,170	1.7%
Machining	266,185	1.9%	249,435	3.2%	16,750	0.3%
Product fabrication, assembling	888,985	6.3%	690,055	8.8%	198,930	3.1%
Construction	843,345	5.9%	820,530	10.5%	22,815	0.4%
Transport equipment operating	508,565	3.6%	461,760	5.9%	46,805	0.7%
Material handling	225,660	1.6%	173,280	2.2%	52,375	0.8%
Other	445,270	3.1%	351,970	4.5%	93,300	1.5%

Source: Statistics Canada, 1991 Census, Catalogue 96-304.

INCOME

Income can be examined at many levels, including individuals, families and households. In addition, Statistics Canada's *Low Income Cut-off* (LICO) is an important indicator of low income. LICOs are determined by analyzing family expenditure data. Families who, on average, spent 20% more of their total income than did the average family on food, shelter and clothing are considered to have low incomes. The LICO for a family of three living in Canada's largest cities was $25,600 in 1993.

Since the 1991 Census, the proportion of families and unattached individuals living with low incomes has increased. In 1990, 12% of families and 38% of unattached individuals had incomes below the LICOs. By 1993, these proportions had increased to 15% of families and 41% of unattached individuals. In addition, average family income in Canada has declined in recent years. From its peak of $57,281 (1993 dollars) in 1989, average family income decreased 7% to $53,459 in 1993. In fact, average family income in 1993, after adjusting for inflation, was slightly lower than the level recorded in 1980 (Income Distributions by Size in Canada, 1993, Statistics Canada Catalogue No. 13-207, 13). In an environment of increased financial pressures on families and individuals, the distribution of income among various groups in society takes on even greater importance.

POPULATION VARIABLES: WHICH GROUPS TO EXAMINE?

Choosing particular sub-groups of the population for analysis is in itself a difficult exercise and entails further value judgments. Some groups have been identified as targets of certain programs or policies. The *Canadian Employment Equity Act*, for example, is aimed at women, visible minorities, aboriginal peoples and persons with disabilities. In addition, the *Canadian Multiculturalism Act* as well as the *Charter of Rights and Freedoms* identify various cultural and ethnic groups in Canadian society. Many other groups, divided along a variety of characteristics, are also of interest and importance: children, youth, seniors, lone-parent families, minority-language groups and immigrants.

Comparing age-based population subgroups (children, youth, adults and seniors) in terms of socio-economic status is difficult, because the indicators of education, employment and income are so closely related to age and the life cycle. Income, for example, is normally low among young people as they complete their schooling and begin their careers. In general, income increases as people advance through their careers, until they enter the retirement stage of their life cycle, when income tends to drop dramatically. Comparisons of income between different age categories, therefore, are often not very meaningful. Also, educational attainment levels have changed so greatly over time that comparisons between young adults and seniors would be inappropriate. For these reasons, age-based subgroups have not been included in this analysis.

Many other groups could also be identified as important in light of social equality and related policy issues. A partial list might include the gay and lesbian population, religious groups and people with disabilities. For some groups, such as gays and lesbians, data is virtually nonexistent. This is unfortunate given the issues of social equality currently being publicly discussed. Some of these issues, such as the recognition of same-sex couples, have recently come before the courts and various legislative bodies in Canada (*The Globe and Mail* 26 May 1995, A14, B18).

That membership in different groups in society can either be beneficial or impose obstacles to "getting ahead" in life is perceived as being important is substantiated in the results of the Canadian portion of the International Social Survey Programme (ISSP). For example, 14% of Canadian respondents to the 1992 survey thought that *gender* was an essential or very important factor in determining one's success in life (see Appendix). Another 21% said that gender was "fairly important" in this regard. Similarly, 11% thought that *race* was essential or very important, and 23% thought race was a fairly important determinant of social mobility. *Education*, however, was almost universally believed to be important; 84% thought it essential or very important (see Appendix).

Respondents to the Canadian sample of the ISSP considered aboriginal peoples to be suffering the most seriously from inequality. Results indicate that 44% felt issues of inequality for aboriginal peoples were very serious and 33% thought them somewhat serious. (See chapters 5 and 6 of this volume for more detailed analysis of this point.) Inequality issues regarding women and visible minorities were also considered to be serious by ISSP respondents. Women's inequality was considered very serious by 24% and somewhat serious by 43% (see chapter 7 of this volume). Issues of inequality as they affect visible minorities were thought very serious by 19% of respondents and 45% said that these issues were somewhat serious. When asked what group should constitute the top priority for action to change the situation of inequality in Canada, 40% of ISSP respondents identified aboriginal peoples, 24% said women and 7% said visible minorities. Only 4% stated that there was no inequality in Canadian society and, therefore, did not identify any group for policy considerations.

Thus, three groups are highlighted in this chapter: women, aboriginal peoples, and visible minorities. Although far from comprehensive, the analysis of these sub-groups of the Canadian population addresses many of the issues touched upon by the ISSP questionnaire and by other chapters in this volume. Using official data sources such as the Census, the

Labour Force Survey and the Aboriginal Peoples Survey, this paper undertakes to describe what is known about the relative socio-economic status
of these groups. In this manner, an empirical context for the ensuing discussions of social inequality based on the ISSP will have been set.

WOMEN IN CANADA

Women constitute 51% of Canada's population. One of the most important social developments of this century has been women's increased
participation in the labour force. Despite having education levels higher
than at any other point in history, women continue to be concentrated in
less desirable jobs and earn substantially less than men. In addition, even
among women who are working, many have primary responsibility for
child-care and other domestic tasks (Frederick, 1955, 55-56).

Women are more educated than ever before. In 1991, 42% of women
aged 15 and over had at least some postsecondary education. As recently
as 1981, this proportion was only 34%. The proportion of women with
a non-university diploma or a professional certificate doubled from 11%
in 1981 to 22% in 1991. Over the same period, the proportion of women
who had a university degree increased from 6% to 10%. In comparison,
13% of men had university degrees in 1991. This situation appears to be
changing, however, as women today account for the majority of students
entering university. At the graduate studies level, women are still a minority.

Level of educational attainment is closely related to employment, particularly among women. In 1991, the employment rate for women having
less than a grade nine education was 19%, while the rate for men with the
same level of education was 39%. At higher levels of educational attainment, however, the gap between men and women closes. In fact, among
women aged 15 to 24 with a university degree, 77% were employed, compared with only 71% of men that age with a degree. In terms of educational
attainment, women have made significant gains in recent years.

The increased presence of women in the workplace is one of the most
important social trends of recent decades. In 1971, only about 40% of
women aged 15 and over were in the labour force (i.e., were working or
looking for work). By 1991, this proportion had increased to 60%. Men's
labour force participation rate, in comparison, remained relatively stable
over the same period. In 1991, the participation rate for men stood at
77%, still substantially higher than that of women. Age is also an important factor, in that younger women are more likely to be active in the

labour force than are older women. In 1991, 79% of women aged 25 to 34 and 80% of those aged 35 to 44 were in the labour force. The comparable rate for women aged 45 to 54 was only 72%. To some extent, this is related to differences in education levels and expectations regarding family responsibility between age groups.

Of course, women still assume primary responsibility for raising children, and this continues to be reflected in labour force participation rates. Among women aged 25 to 34, for example, 91% of those without children were in the labour force, compared with 70% of women who did have children at home. This relationship is even more evident among women with young children: 67% of women aged 25 to 34 with at least one child under age 6 were active in the labour force. In 1981, just 10 years earlier, the labour force participation rate of women aged 25 to 34 with at least one pre-school aged child was just 49%. The increased participation of mothers seems to have prompted improvements in the availability of child-care and in the flexibility of work schedules, which in turn has facilitated further participation.

Unemployment is slightly lower among women than among men. Among people who are part of the labour force, the unemployment rate has exhibited an upward trend for both women and men since the mid-1960s. According to the Labour Force Survey, in 1993 11% of women and 12% of men wanted to work but were unable to find a job. This difference between women and men was most pronounced among young workers. Among those aged 15 to 24, unemployment was 20% for men and only 15% for women. In comparison, 11% of men and 10% of women aged 25 to 44, and 9% of both men and women aged 45 to 64 were unemployed in 1993.

Part-time work has been on the increase in recent years. In 1993, 17% of people with jobs had only part-time work, up from 11% in 1975. Part-time work is more common among women than it is among men (Best, 1955, 32-33). In 1993, 26% of employed women worked part-time, compared with only 10% of employed men. For many people, especially women, part-time work may be a matter of choice, because it allows them to balance work with other responsibilities. For others, however, part-time work is a necessity, because full-time work cannot be found. Of women who were working part-time in 1993, 34% did so because it was the only work they could find, 32% did not want full-time work, 21% were going to school, and 11% did so because of personal or family responsibilities. This last reason was cited by only 1% of men who were working part-time.

Many women still work in jobs that have traditionally been performed by women. Clerical work, for example, accounted for 28% of working women's jobs in 1993. This was down, however, from 34% in 1982. Over the same period, the proportion of women working in managerial and administrative occupations grew to 13% from 6%. Perhaps the most visible area of progress made by women in the working world has been in the professions. In 1982, for example, women accounted for only 18% of doctors and dentists. By 1993, this proportion had increased to 26%. Women made up 42% of all people in managerial and administrative positions in 1993, up from 29% in 1982. Similarly, over the same period, the proportion of women working in social sciences or religion grew to 56% from 43%. Self-employment is also increasing among women. Ten percent of women were self-employed in 1993, up from 7% in 1981. The most common occupations of self-employed women were in the areas of child-care, sales, book-keeping and accounting services, and personal care services. Still, men (20%) are much more likely than women to be self-employed.

Women continue to earn substantially less than men. Even after taking part-time work into account, women's earnings are considerably lower. Nonetheless, this situation is changing. With higher levels of education and work experience, an increased proportion of women are occupying well-paying jobs. Women who were employed full-time throughout 1993 earned an average of $28,390. This represented 72% of the earnings of men who were employed full-time throughout the year ($39,430). The male/female earnings gap has narrowed considerably since 1989, when full-time earnings of women were 66% of those of men, and from 1975, when the figure was 60%.

When one examines the status of women in Canada today compared to a century or even half a century ago, the magnitude of the social change that has taken place over this relatively short period becomes evident. At the beginning of the twentieth century, Canadian women did not have the right to vote in federal elections, were not generally active in the paid labour force, and were excluded from many aspects of the social and economic life of the country. Laws, policies and customs were established and perpetuated largely by men for a male-dominated society.

Although women have made dramatic gains in many areas, it would be premature to say that social equality between the sexes has been achieved. Women are still less likely than men to be in the labour force, and continue to bear the brunt of family responsibilities, whether or not they are working. Even among those who do participate in the paid work force, women continue to be concentrated in low-paying jobs and are more likely than men to work only part-time. All indicators, however, point to a continued narrowing of the gaps between men and women in terms of education, employment and income.

In summary, women have made significant progress in terms of the indicators examined. Women are more educated than ever before and, in recent years, have accounted for a majority of university enrolments. Labour force participation among women has increased steadily since 1971 and more women are in well-paying jobs, including professional occupations. Consequently, evidence of these changes can be seen in the earnings gap between men and women, which is gradually closing.

ABORIGINAL PEOPLES

Aboriginal peoples comprise a unique group in Canada. As North America's original inhabitants, their marginalized status in Canadian society is cause for serious concern. Under the *Constitution Act, 1867*, the federal government has jurisdiction to make laws in relation to aboriginal peoples. Although Canadian law distinguishes between status and non-status Indians, the 1991 Aboriginal Peoples Survey (upon which most of this section is based) defined its target population as those who identify with an aboriginal group, regardless of their legal status. The survey estimated that there were nearly 400,000 people aged 15 and over who identified with an aboriginal group in 1991.

Aboriginal people tend to have less formal education than the Canadian population as a whole. In 1991, 17% of aboriginal people aged 15 to 49 had less than a Grade 9 education or had no formal schooling at all. Among the total Canadian population that age, only 6% had less than Grade 9 or had no formal schooling. Similarly, 33% of people who identified with an aboriginal group, and who were aged 15 to 49, reported having some postsecondary education (including those with a university degree), compared with 51% of the general population that age.

In the case of aboriginal peoples, access to elementary and secondary schools was not necessarily beneficial. Residential school systems run by religious organizations were in operation until the early 1980s. Abuse of student residents and the suppression of aboriginal culture that took place in these schools has since been well documented. According to the Aboriginal Peoples Survey, 11% of aboriginal people aged 15 to 49 who attended elementary school lived in residential schools for all or part of their elementary schooling. Similarly, 10% of those who attended secondary school lived in residential schools for at least part of that phase of their education. Education in all types of schools was often not culturally sensitive to the needs of aboriginal students. Among those aged 15 to 49, 23% had aboriginal teachers at some point during elementary school, and 15% had aboriginal teachers during secondary school. Only 11% reported that they had been taught in an aboriginal language at any stage of their elementary schooling. The proportion was only 6% at the secondary level.

Even so, almost 40% of aboriginal people aged 15 to 49 reported having been taught about aboriginal people while in elementary school. Of these, 87% liked what they were taught. In secondary school, 35% had been taught about aboriginal people and 87% of them enjoyed this part of their education. The degree to which this situation has changed can be measured to some extent by examining the same indicators for both older and younger aboriginal people. Among those aged 50 to 64, 53% reported no formal schooling or having less than a Grade 9 education, compared with 26% of the general population that age. Only 22% of aboriginal people aged 50 to 64 reported having some postsecondary education (including a university degree), compared with 33% of all Canadians that age. Of aboriginal people aged 50 to 64 who attended elementary and/or secondary school, more than one-third had lived in residential schools for all or part of that time.

The situation is quite different for aboriginal children today. Among those aged 5 to 14 (and who had the corresponding level of education), only 1% had lived in an elementary residential school and 4% had lived in a secondary residential school. This system of schooling has now been completely dismantled and children entering the school system today are not exposed to residential schools. In fact, of the aboriginal children surveyed in 1991, 92% of those who were in or had gone to elementary school lived with their families while doing so.

The proportion of aboriginal children who had aboriginal teachers is now higher. Among those aged 5 to 14, 40% had elementary and 18% had secondary teachers who were aboriginal. Similarly, larger proportions of these aboriginal children reported having been taught in an aboriginal language at some time. This was the case for 25% of those who had attended elementary school and 9% of those who had been to secondary school.

Aboriginal peoples had lower rates of labour force participation and employment than other Canadians. In the week before the 1991 Census, the labour force participation rate for aboriginal peoples aged 15 and over was 57%, compared with 68% for all Canadians. Among labour force participants, the unemployment rate for people who identified with an aboriginal group was 25%. This was 2.5 times the rate for the general population.

Of all adults who identified with an aboriginal group, 59% worked for income in 1990 and/or 1991. In addition to regular paid work, many aboriginal people were engaged in other activities for pay. Nearly one-fifth of those aged 15 and over reported activities such as trapping, guiding, or arts and crafts for which they earned money. Furthermore, 14% reported activities to support themselves and their families such as fishing, hunting or trading for food for which they did not receive money. For many, the "bush economy" is an important component of aboriginal life that is not normally captured by conventional labour force concepts.

Of the total adult population that identified with an aboriginal group, one-third were looking for work at some point during 1990 and/or 1991. Of these people, nearly two-thirds reported having difficulty finding work because there were few or no jobs available, and 41% said that their education and job experience did not match the type of work that was available. About 16% said they had difficulty finding work because they were aboriginal people.

Incomes, from all sources, of people who identify with an aboriginal group are dramatically lower than those of the Canadian population in general. For example, while 15% of Canadians aged 15 and over had incomes of $40,000 or more, this was the case for only 5% of aboriginal people that age. At the other extreme, 13% of aboriginal adults had no income and 12% had incomes of less than $2,000 in 1990. That year, 9% of all Canadian adults had no income and only 6% had incomes of less than $2,000. Nearly one-half (47%) of people who identified with an aboriginal group had employment incomes of less than $20,000, compared with 29% of the general population.

In 1990, 29% of aboriginal people aged 15 and over received social assistance. Of these, 65% reported having received social assistance for a period of six months or more during that year. An even higher proportion of aboriginal people who live on reserves are social assistance beneficiaries. According to Indian and Northern Affairs Canada, an average of 38% of on-reserve aboriginal people received social assistance between 1981 and

1992. Over the same period, the average proportion of people across Canada receiving social assistance (excluding aboriginal people living on reserves) was only 7% (*Report of the Auditor General of Canada to the House of Commons*, 1994, volume 14, Chapter 23, 9).

Many aboriginal communities face serious challenges, as their residents do not participate in the economic life of the country as fully as do other Canadians. The reasons for this are complex, and can be traced to Canada's colonial history and the various policy approaches taken by governments over time. A partial list of the problems facing aboriginal communities includes unemployment, family violence, substance abuse, suicide, disease and poor housing conditions. According to aboriginal peoples themselves, problems in their communities and neighbourhoods could be overcome in a variety of ways. The Aboriginal Peoples Survey asked respondents to list the approaches they felt would improve their situations. The most commonly given response was that things could be improved by having widely available family service counselling and other non-family counselling services. Having more policing and improved community services were the approaches next most frequently cited. Finally, providing more employment and improved education were also suggested as approaches to overcoming the problems facing aboriginal communities and neighbourhoods.

To apply the notion of inequality to the situation of aboriginal peoples is to state the obvious. Here is a group in Canadian society that historically has faced assimilation and paternalism. That aboriginal peoples have not only survived, but have extended their social, economic and political aspirations to the extent that they have in the face of such adversity is testament to their resilience as a people. As aboriginal peoples continue to negotiate land claims settlements and educate their children in what would appear to be a renaissance of aboriginal culture, the prospects for breaking the cycle of dependency seem good. The extent to which the nature and level of aboriginal peoples' participation in the economic life of the country will improve remains to be seen.

VISIBLE MINORITIES

People in visible minorities constitute one of the four designated populations identified in the *Employment Equity Act*, 1986. According to the *Act*, visible minorities include persons, other than aboriginal peoples, who are non-Caucasian in race and non-white in colour (Interdepartmental

Working Group on Employment Equity Data. *Women, Visible Minorities, Aboriginal Peoples and Persons with Disabilities: The 1991 Employment Equity Definitions.* Ottawa, 1993). In 1991, the 1.9 million people aged 15 and over who were in a visible minority group accounted for 9% of the total adult population in Canada. People in visible minorities tend to live in urban areas. In fact, in 1991, 69% lived in Canada's three largest cities alone (40% in Toronto, 15% in Vancouver, and 14% in Montreal).

Most people in visible minorities were not born in Canada. In 1991, 78% were immigrants and an additional 7% were non-permanent residents. This is important, because differences between groups in terms of socio-economic status are influenced by other factors, such as period of arrival and knowledge of official languages. Also, the age structures of people in these different groups vary considerably. South East Asians and Latin Americans tend to be younger than people in other visible minority groups and other Canadians. Japanese, Koreans, and Chinese people tend to be older. Differing age structures account for some of the differences observed in indicators of socio-economic status.

Taken as a group, people in visible minorities are better educated than are non-visible minority Canadians. For example, 18% of people in visible minorities who were aged 15 and over had a university degree in 1991, compared with 11% of the non-visible minority population and of the adult Canadian population as a whole. Similarly, only 12% of people in visible minorities had less than Grade 9 education, compared with 14% among people who were not part of a visible minority group.

Within visible minority groups, however, the level of education varies greatly, with more established groups generally having higher educational attainment than other groups. For example, 27% of Koreans, 26% of Filipinos, 24% of West Asians and 23% of Japanese people held a university degree in 1991. At the other end of the educational spectrum, relatively small proportions of people in these groups had less than a Grade 9 education (5% of Koreans and Japanese people, 6% of Filipinos and 11% of West Asians). South East Asians (21%), Chinese people (16%) and Latin Americans (15%), on the other hand, were the most likely to have less than a Grade 9 education, and university degrees were held by only 10% of South East Asians and by 11% of Latin Americans. Even after taking differences in age structure between the groups into account, the same pattern of differences in educational attainment among visible minority groups is evident (Kelly, 1995, 5-6).

Also, significant differences exist between men and women in these groups. Among South East Asians, for example, 26% of women have less than a Grade 9 education, compared with only 16% of their male counterparts. Similarly, the proportion of men with a university degree is consistently higher than that of women across all visible minority groups. Still, these proportions for men and women in visible minority groups are generally higher than are those for non-visible minority men and women.

TABLE 2: PROPORTION OF PEOPLE
WITH A UNIVERSITY DEGREE, 1991

	Total	Men	Women
Non-visible minorities	11%	12%	9%
All visible minorities	18%	21%	15%
Korean	27%	33%	21%
Filipino	26%	24%	27%
West Asian	24%	28%	19%
Japanese	23%	26%	20%
Chinese	21%	25%	16%
South Asian	19%	23%	16%
Multiple visible minorities	16%	17%	15%
Latin American	11%	13%	10%
South East Asian	10%	13%	8%
Black	10%	12%	8%
Other Pacific	10%	10%	10%

Source: Statistics Canada, Employment Equity Program.

These gender differences are generally much more pronounced than for the Canadian population as a whole. The fact that many visible minority persons are immigrants partially explains these differences. Many women may not have had access to postsecondary education in their home countries. In addition, for some groups, cultural factors, both in their original countries and in Canada, may play a role in inhibiting women's access to higher education.

Labour force participation among people in visible minorities is slightly higher than it is among other Canadians. In 1991, 77% of men and 64% of women who were in a visible minority were either employed or actively seeking work, compared with 76% of men and 59% of women who were not in a visible minority category. However, age-standardization lowers the labour force participation rates of people in visible minorities. After taking age into account, 74% of visible minority men and 59% of visible minority women were active in the labour force (Kelly, 1995, 6).

TABLE 3: LABOUR FORCE PARTICIPATION
AND EMPLOYMENT, 1991

	Labour Force Participation Rate (%)			Unemployment Rate (%)		
	Total	Men	Women	Total	Men	Women
Non-visible minorities	68	76	59	10	10	10
All visible minorities	70	77	64	13	13	13
Korean	68	75	61	8	8	8
Filipino	80	80	80	7	8	5
West Asian	67	77	55	17	16	19
Japanese	66	74	57	6	6	7
Chinese	67	73	60	10	9	11
South Asian	74	82	66	14	12	17
Multiple visible minorities	75	80	70	11	10	21
Latin American	67	76	58	20	19	21
South East Asian	67	74	58	17	16	18
Black	73	78	69	15	16	14
Other pacific	76	82	71	9	8	9

Source: Statistics Canada, Employment Equity Program.

Thus, while the rates for visible minority and other women were the same, visible minority men were actually slightly less likely to be in the labour force than other Canadian men.

Considerable variation in labour force participation rates exists between different visible minority groups. In 1991, 80% of Filipinos were in the labour force, compared with 66% of Japanese and 67% of West Asian, South-east Asian, Chinese, and Latin American people. Again, varying age structures have an impact on these differences. The Japanese, for example, are the oldest visible minority group and also exhibit the lowest labour force participation rate.

Although a relatively high proportion of people in visible minority groups are in the labour force, these people have higher rates of unemployment than do other Canadians. In 1991, unemployment among people in visible minorities was 13%, compared with 10% among people who were not in a visible minority. Again, there was considerable variation between groups. Unemployment ranged from a low of 6% among Japanese people to a high of 20% among people in the Latin American visible minority group.

When visible minorities' incomes were examined, only full-time workers who worked throughout 1990 were included. In this manner, the effect of differences in the proportion of groups working only part-time were eliminated. Overall, people in visible minorities earned less than did other Canadians. The average annual income of people in visible minorities was $30,129 in 1990, compared with $34,049 among non-visible minorities.

The average annual income of most visible minority groups was lower than that of non-visible minorities. Japanese people, however, had an average annual income ($41,235) that was higher than the average for people in non-visible minorities. All other visible minority groups had average annual incomes that were lower than those of other Canadians.

TABLE 4: AVERAGE ANNUAL INCOME,
FULL-TIME, FULL-YEAR WORKERS, 1990

	Total	Men	Women
Non-visible minorities	$34,049	$39,023	$26,204
All visible minorities	$30,129	$34,376	$24,359
Korean	$28,436	$32,514	$23,235
Filipino	$25,619	$30,739	$22,574
West Asian	$33,138	$36,312	$25,875
Japanese	$41,235	$48,273	$30,157
Chinese	$30,914	$34,846	$25,448
South Asian	$31,492	$35,834	$24,155
Multiple visible minorities	$30,230	$34,116	$25,556
Latin American	$24,760	$27,674	$20,285
South East Asian	$25,370	$28,117	$20,673
Black	$28,850	$32,898	$24,412
Other Pacific	$30,515	$34,721	$25,506

Source: Statistics Canada, Employment Equity Program.

People in visible minorities comprise a diverse group, which makes generalization difficult. The number of variables influencing levels of education, labour force participation, and income make the subject worthy of a much more detailed analysis than that presented here. Factors including age, experience, language, and period of arrival vary considerably among the different visible minority groups.

◆

This chapter has examined women, aboriginal peoples and visible minorities in terms of several indicators of socio-economic status, including education, employment and income. Women are considerably less likely than men to be in the labour force. Women are, however, more educated than ever before, and the salary gap between men and women has been narrowing. This trend is likely to continue, as women today account for the majority of students enrolled in university. With higher levels of education and accumulated experience, women are increasingly occuying more highly qualified, better-paying jobs. Nonetheless, many women still encounter barriers to further participation and hit a so-called "glass ceiling" that is indicative of continuing structural inequality.

The differences in socio-economic status between aboriginal peoples and the Canadian population in general are striking. Aboriginal peoples have relatively low levels of educational attainment and this has filtered down to employment patterns and ultimately to income. Aboriginal peoples are not participating in the economic life of Canada to the same extent as other Canadians. With visible minorities the situation is more difficult to analyze. When we examine raw indicators of education, employment and income, some visible minority groups are clearly better off than others. As a whole, visible minorities participate less fully in the work force than do other Canadians. The situation, however, cannot be examined quite that simply. One must take into account a myriad of factors when looking at the relative socio-economic status of visible minority groups. Because many visible minorities are recent immigrants to Canada, other factors, such as period of arrival and knowledge of official languages, are extremely important.

Inequality in terms of socio-economic status does exist. Survey data such as those utilized in this paper are useful in providing a snapshot of the relative socio-economic status of people in these various groups. The main data sources used here have been the Census, the Aboriginal Peoples Survey and the Labour Force Survey. In addition, attitudinal data such as those collected in the 1992 cycle of the International Social Survey Programme are also important in furthering understanding of people's perceptions of inequality, and add an international dimension. Soon, the results of longitudinal surveys, including Statistics Canada's Survey of Labour and Income Dynamics and the National Longitudinal Survey of Children, will also contribute to our understanding of social inequality.

The Survey of Labour and Income Dynamics (SLID) will generate data on individuals over time to track their mobility, educational development, labour market experiences, and changes in their income and family circumstances. These data will facilitate the examination of the factors that work together to influence employment and income. Data from SLID will also allow longitudinal research on the changing nature and extent of poverty among individuals and families along various characteristics, including gender and ethnicity. In 1993, the survey began tracking the experiences of 16,000 households for a six-year period. A new panel of households will join the survey every three years.

The National Longitudinal Survey of Children (NLSC) is designed to examine how children's upbringing, their home and school experiences influence their development and behaviour throughout childhood and into adult life. A national database of Canadian children will open new dimensions of research not previously possible. The NLSC is certain to produce new insights into the complex combination of factors that affect a person's social and economic well-being. With these and other new surveys, the study of social inequality will have some powerful new tools.

REFERENCES

Best, Pamela. (1995). Women, Men and Work. *Canadian Social Trends*, Spring, Statistics Canada Catalogue No. 11-008, No. 36.

Frederick, Judith A. (1995). *As Time Goes By ... Time Use of Canadians*, General Social Survey, Statistics Canada Catalogue No. 89-544.

Kelly, Karen. (1995). Visible Minorities: A Diverse Group. *Canadian Social Trends*, Summer, Statistics Canada Catalogue 11-008, No. 37.

STATISTICS CANADA PUBLICATIONS

Statistics Canada, *Educational Attainment and School Attendance*, Catalogue No. 93-328. Ottawa: Minister of Industry, Science and Technology, 1993.

————, *Employment Income by Occupation*, Catalogue No. 93-328. Ottawa: Minister of Industry, Science and Technology, 1993.

————, *Historical Labour Force Statistics*, 1994, Catalogue No. 71-201. Ottawa: Minister of Industry, Science and Technology, 1995.

————, *Housing and Other Characteristics of Canadian Households*, Catalogue No. 93-330. Ottawa: Minister of Industry, Science and Technology, 1993.

Statistics Canada, *Labour Force Activity,* Catalogue No. 93-324. Ottawa: Minister of Industry, Science and Technology, 1993.

———, *Language, Tradition, Health, Lifestyle and Social Issues,* 1991 Aboriginal Peoples Survey, Catalogue No. 89-533. Ottawa: Minister of Industry, Science and Technology, 1993.

———, *Occupation,* Catalogue No. 93-327. Ottawa: Minister of Industry, Science and Technology, 1993.

———, *Schooling, Work and Related Activities, Income, Expenses and Mobility,* 1991 Aboriginal Peoples Survey, Catalogue No. 89-534. Ottawa: Minister of Industry, Science and Technology, 1993.

———, *Selected Income Statistics,* Catalogue No. 93-331. Ottawa: Minister of Industry, Science and Technology, 1993.

———, *Women in Canada: A Statistical Report, Third Edition,* Catalogue No. 89-503. Ottawa: Minister of Industry, 1995.

———, *Women in the Labour Force,* 1994 Edition, Catalogue No. 75-507. Ottawa: Minister of Industry, Science and Technology, 1994.

CHAPTER THREE

INTERNATIONAL IMAGES OF SOCIAL INEQUALITY
A TEN-COUNTRY COMPARISON

Carl J. Cuneo

GLOBAL SOCIETY at the end of the twentieth, and beginning of the twenty-first, century is rapidly moving toward social, economic, and political integration. The rapidity of this development has created many clashes and difficulties for nation-states as well as for groups, organizations, and citizens of individual countries. One of these is the persistence, if not the increase, in the extent and depth of social inequality, both between nations and among peoples within each country. The combination of persistent inequalities and global integration presents both challenges and opportunities for social scientists. The opportunities lie in the greater potential for collaborative research between countries. This is enabled especially by developments in communications technology. Social and political researchers used to work relatively independently on questions of inequality at the local, regional, and national levels within their own countries. Using common measures and theoretical approaches, there is now the opportunity to create common global projects focused on international similarities and differences in social inequality. But this brings new challenges not confronted to the same degree in local and regional research. Not only do we have to sort out the clash of competing theoretical assumptions and perspectives on a wider global scale, but also, if our interpretations are to be valid, the measures we use must be sensitive to national cultural meanings, while simultaneously having sufficient similarity to allow for valid international comparison. This is not an easy task when one entertains the nuances of linguistic meanings attached to words in different national and regional cultures.

Some progress has been made in this direction among political scientists researching subjective constructions of images of social inequality between countries (Evans, 1993; Hayes, 1995). On the assumption that "a picture is worth a thousand words," and graphics can sometimes convey clearer, more immediate and direct messages than text or words, researchers have constructed five pictures of the profiles of social inequalities that might characterize different societies (Evans, Kelly, & Kolosi, 1992, 462-65). These typically take the form of layered rectangles of different widths representing the proportion of people in the society at different levels of social hierarchies. Using such graphics, profiles have been constructed of the egalitarian society (a large middle and smaller upper and lower levels); a lower middle-class society (a large layer below the middle and progressively smaller layers at the bottom and top); an upper middle-class society (a larger layer just above the middle, with progressively smaller ones at the top and bottom); a pyramid society (progressively wider rectangles from top to bottom); and, an elite/mass society (a small upper crust, a larger mass at the bottom, and small layers in the middle).

The purpose of this chapter is to examine international differences in perceptions of such systems of inequality selected by citizens to characterize their societies in the present, past, and future; as well, we include their morally preferred structures with no particular time reference.[1] Past research has shown that, despite selecting a model characterizing their present societies as sharply unequal, many people hope for a more egalitarian future (Evans, Kelly, & Kolosi, 1992). We will seek to explain some of the social origins of the inequality models selected by citizens. These deal mainly with objective structures of class and stratification, and gender and age inequalities. Following Evans, Kelly, and Kolosi (1992), we hypothesize that those at the bottom of various socio-economic scales will more likely see society as one of deep cleavages of inequalities, while the more privileged are likely to select more egalitarian images of society. We also examine the contribution of objective and subjective inequalities for the potential of conflict in society. Our hypothesis is that the disinherited, and those subscribing to elite/mass dichotomous models, will be the most likely to view society in terms of six kinds of group conflict (see Kelly & Evans, 1995). At the end of the paper, we consider how well those with low socio-economic status are represented in such research. The sources of data for this chapter are the same as the others in this book—the 1992 International Social Survey Programme (ISSP).

SUBJECTIVE CLASS RANKINGS OF COUNTRIES

In the economics, politics, and development literatures, the countries of the world are ranked in terms of power, economic resources, and the quality of life, all central features of social inequality. These rankings are usually based on collective properties of nation-states. However, they usually have a subjective side, in that the citizens of each country place themselves higher or lower on various subjective scales of stratification and social class. The result is that citizens in economically more developed countries will, on average, place themselves higher on subjective scales of inequality than citizens in less developed countries. The breakup of the communist bloc countries, and dramatic changes in their political and economic structures, make this topic especially pertinent as nations sort themselves out in the new system of international social inequality.

In Table 1, the percent distribution and mean rankings of respondents in the 1992 ISSP survey on subjective social class are shown for 18 countries. To facilitate understanding, the countries are ranked from the top to bottom of the table by their mean score on a subjective social class question. Respondents in the country surveys were asked, "In our society there are groups which tend to be towards the top and groups which tend to be towards the bottom. Below is a scale that runs from top to bottom. Where would you put yourself on this scale?" Respondents were presented with a ladder on which they placed themselves from steps 1 to 10. Responses were recoded and divided into three categories: upper (7 to 10), middle (4 to 6), and lower (1 to 3). The mean and standard deviations in the last two columns are based on scores from 1 (lowest) to 10 (highest).

Four clusters of countries are highlighted. The breaks between the clusters are at least 0.29; this is greater than the differences between any two sequential pair of countries within the clusters. New Zealand has the highest ranking (5.99); Bulgaria the lowest (3.84). Generally, the highest rankings are held by advanced industrial and post-industrial countries in Group I from the West and South Pacific (New Zealand, Australia, Norway, Canada, Austria, West Germany, Sweden, the United States, and Great Britain). Their ranks are within the narrow and high range of 5.99 to 5.34. Group II, the next highest, is dominated by former Eastern

TABLE 1: SUBJECTIVE CLASS,* BY COUNTRY, 1992

Rank Order	Country	Percent Distribution:**			Mean Rank (1=bottom; 10=top)	Standard Deviation of Mean Ranks
		Upper (7-10)	Middle (4-6)	Lower (1-3)		
1	New Zealand	38	52	10	5.99	1.74
2	Australia	27	64	8	5.88	1.44
3	Norway	32	59	8	5.85	1.55
4	Canada	34	56	10	5.83	1.77
5	Austria	27	64	9	5.77	1.54
6	West Germany	30	61	9	5.72	1.54
7	Sweden	31	59	10	5.70	1.76
8	USA	27	59	14	5.54	1.83
9	Great Britain	24	61	15	5.34	1.79
10	Italy	13	67	20	4.94	1.67
11	Slovakia	11	64	25	4.77	1.78
12	East Germany	11	65	24	4.71	1.60
13	Czech Republic	11	64	25	4.69	1.68
14	Russia	9	60	31	4.40	1.84
15	Philippines	9	61	30	4.36	1.88
16	Poland	10	54	36	4.32	1.93
17	Hungary	5	56	39	3.92	1.60
18	Bulgaria	4	51	45	3.84	1.76

Eta = .389
Eta^2 = .151

chi square: p <.001

* "In our society there are groups which tend to be towards the top and groups which tend to be towards the bottom. Below is a scale that runs from top to bottom. Where would you put yourself on this scale?" (from 1 to 10).
** Percentages may not total 100 because of rounding errors.

European communist nations—Slovakia, East Germany, and the Czech Republic. Italy is the only western European nation in this group; not surprisingly it is at the top of this category, with a score of 4.94, considerably less than the lowest country in Group I (Great Britain, with a score of 5.34). Group III contains two ex-communist bloc countries (Russia and Poland) and one developing country (Republic of the Philippines). At the bottom of the rankings is Group IV, containing two countries—Hungary and Bulgaria.

Differences among these four groups are also meaningful in terms of the placements in the upper and lowest ranks on the 10-point subjective class scale. In Group I, 24 to 38% of all respondents in nine countries place themselves in the highest four ranks (from 7 to 10); this drops dramatically in Group II (11 to 13 %), Group III (9 to 10%), and Group

IV (4 to 5%). In contrast, very few residents in Group I countries place themselves at the bottom of the subjective social scale (only 8 to 15% place themselves in the bottom 1 to 3 rank positions). This rises to a level between 20 and 25% in Group II, 30 to 36% in Group III, and 39 to 45% in Group IV.

While these rankings would be externally and highly correlated with objective measures of the collective economic resources and political power of these nations, they also have a bearing on the internal perceptions of the profiles of the structures of social inequality held within each country. It is to this topic that we devote the rest of the chapter. After outlining the structure of five different profiles of inequality, we will examine some of their roots, their bearing on perceptions of social conflict, and finally the capacity of respondents to cope with such questions in terms of their socio-economic characteristics.

SUBJECTIVE PROFILES OF SOCIAL INEQUALITY

People may place themselves at different locations in a structure of inequality, and they may use different criteria in doing so. One of the most difficult issues in cross-comparative survey research is the comparability of interview and questionnaire items, and hence of measures. Each country may have a unique sense of its structure of social inequality in terms of income, occupational structure, status, and class. Additionally, linguistic differences in the meaning of words can erect formidable barriers to comparisons of similar items between countries. One partial solution to these problems is the use of pictures or graphics during the interview, accompanied by oral or written questions. As evidenced in the common recognition of international traffic signs (such as the "triangle" for "yield" and the "octagon" for "stop"), the use of such symbols in social research may facilitate common understandings and interpretations of questions across a wide range of national cultures.

The rest of this chapter utilizes one such example of the use of graphics in interviews, in a program of research on perceptions of social inequality. Respondents in the ISSP survey were presented with five alternative profiles of their country's structure of social inequality, and asked to choose among them. One of these profiles is shown at the top of each of the following tables. A description of each was read to the respondents as follows:

- **Elite/Mass**: "Type A: The small elite at the top, very few people in the middle and the great mass of people at the bottom."
- **Pyramid**: "Type B: A society like a pyramid, with a small elite at the top, more people in the middle, and most at the bottom."
- **Lower-Middle**: "Type C: A pyramid except that just a few people are at the very bottom."
- **Middle**: "Type D: A society with most of the people in the middle."
- **Upper-Middle**: "Type E: Many people near the top and only a few near the bottom."

Respondents were asked which diagram:

- came closest to describing their society *today*,
- their best guess in describing society *30 years ago* (in the 1960s),
- their best guess in describing society *30 years from now*, and
- what they *prefer* their society *ought to be*.

The percentage of respondents choosing each diagram or profile of inequality for these four periods are shown in Tables 2 to 6.[2] This question was asked only in the following ten countries: Hungary, the Czech Republic, Poland, Bulgaria, Italy, Norway, Canada, New Zealand, Australia and the Republic of the Philippines. Each table corresponds to one of the five profiles.

TABLE 2: PERCENT OF RESPONDENTS
SELECTING **Type A: Elite/Mass**
SOCIAL STRUCTURE IN SELECTED
HISTORICAL PERIODS, BY COUNTRY, 1992

| Country | Historical Period | | | Morally Preferred Structure |
	30 years ago	Now	30 years from now	
Hungary	18	50	23	1
Czech Republic	19	28	16	1
Poland	25	58	23	3
Bulgaria	14	59	15	1
Italy	45	14	16	3
Norway	15	8	14	1
Canada	17	23	40	2
New Zealand	5	24	35	1
Australia	20	15	26	1
Philippines	19	44	22	12

TABLE 3: PERCENT OF RESPONDENTS
SELECTING **Type B: Pyramid**
SOCIAL STRUCTURE IN SELECTED
HISTORICAL PERIODS, BY COUNTRY, 1992

| Country | Historical Period | | | Morally Preferred Structure |
	30 years ago	Now	30 years from now	
Hungary	26	32	11	5
Czech Republic	24	39	15	4
Poland	33	22	17	10
Bulgaria	26	24	16	1
Italy	32	34	16	10
Norway	31	16	26	3
Canada	31	33	23	6
New Zealand	15	39	29	4
Australia	31	32	25	8
Philippines	25	27	22	16

TABLE 4: PERCENT OF RESPONDENTS
SELECTING **Type C: Lower-Middle**
SOCIAL STRUCTURE IN SELECTED
HISTORICAL PERIODS, BY COUNTRY, 1992

| Country | Historical Period | | | Morally Preferred Structure |
	30 years ago	Now	30 years from now	
Hungary	22	7	15	16
Czech Republic	20	12	18	17
Poland	15	7	15	7
Bulgaria	21	6	18	4
Italy	11	21	18	13
Norway	30	25	21	7
Canada	21	21	13	10
New Zealand	26	23	15	13
Australia	21	27	18	14
Philippines	25	10	18	14

Several striking patterns emerge from the tables (which should be read together).

First, the most popular profiles in terms of preference, or the direction in which respondents think society is moving, are the middle and upper-middle models in Tables 5 and 6. This may be taken as a symbol of the strain toward equality, or at least a social structure that has a large upper-middle class into which the majority of those below can potentially move.

TABLE 5: PERCENT OF RESPONDENTS
SELECTING **Type D: Middle** SOCIAL
STRUCTURE IN SELECTED HISTORICAL PERIODS,
BY COUNTRY, 1992

| Country | Historical Period | | | Morally Preferred Structure |
	30 years ago	Now	30 years from now	
Hungary	28	7	29	44
Czech Republic	30	19	32	37
Poland	21	9	30	46
Bulgaria	36	9	33	46
Italy	10	23	32	44
Norway	21	49	31	62
Canada	27	20	19	49
New Zealand	47	13	17	58
Australia	23	24	25	52
Philippines	21	12	23	35

TABLE 6: PERCENT OF RESPONDENTS
SELECTING **Type E: Upper-Middle**
SOCIAL STRUCTURE IN SELECTED HISTORICAL
PERIODS, BY COUNTRY, 1992

| Country | Historical Period | | | Morally Preferred Structure |
	30 years ago	Now	30 years from now	
Hungary	7	3	22	34
Czech Republic	7	3	20	40
Poland	6	4	16	34
Bulgaria	4	1	18	48
Italy	3	8	19	31
Norway	3	2	8	27
Canada	4	2	5	33
New Zealand	8	1	4	24
Australia	5	1	5	26
Philippines	10	8	15	24

Second, with some exceptions respondents seem pessimistic about the society in which they live. They typically characterize it in terms of deep inequalities—either as an elite/mass society in Table 2, or as a pyramid with the majority of people marooned at the bottom in Table 3. One notable exception is Norway, where 49% describe their society today as middle class (Table 5). Very few describe their present society as upper-middle (Table 6).

Third, the pyramid social structure—with the majority at the bottom—shows a steady decrease in popularity in every country from the present, to 30 years hence, to the morally preferred society (see Table 3). This is not surprising, since it is the one social structure that holds out the least hope for upward mobility for the majority of people.

Fourth, the exact reverse is evident in Tables 5 and 6, in which there is a steady increase in support for each of the middle and upper-middle profiles from the present to 30 years hence to the morally preferred society. The only two exceptions are the middle-class profiles in Norway and Canada. Both of these tables thus suggest peoples' hope for greater egalitarianism and upward mobility in the future.

Fifth, there are strong international differences in which inequality profiles citizens select to depict their *present* society. In Table 2, residents of the former eastern communist bloc countries, as well as the Philippines, are more likely than the developed West to characterize their present society in terms of the sharp divisions between a small elite at the top and a large mass at the bottom. In contrast, respondents in the West—especially Canada, Italy, Norway, and Australia—are more likely to view their present society as either the egalitarian middle (Table 5) or the lower-middle (Table 4). This finding is interesting, given the egalitarian ideology that was current among the ex-communist nations. We do not have sufficient time series data to determine whether there was a greater mass sense of egalitarianism before the fall of state communism in Eastern Europe, or whether citizens of these countries are now experiencing deeper inequalities as a result of the rise of market capitalism.

Sixth, across all countries the morally preferred society is the middle class model shown in Table 5. Thirty-five to 62% of respondents in all countries chose this profile over the other four as their preferred society. This seems a clear indication of a majority support in all countries surveyed for an egalitarian society without the extremes of wealth and power concentrated in a few hands, or of the majority confined to the lower reaches of society, unable to advance upward because of the lack of higher structural positions.

ROOTS OF VARIATIONS IN SUBJECTIVE PROFILES

The following propositions have received widespread theoretical and empirical support in the large literature on class and stratification. The working class, and those at the bottom of the socio-economic scale—

whether in terms of occupational status, income, education, or minority gender and ethnic/racial status—will characterize society as having deep inequalities to the advantage of the rich and powerful and the disadvantage of the poor and powerless. They are the most likely to view society as torn between a small class or elite of economically and politically powerful people and a much larger class of working people unable to move upward because of the lack of positions in the middle. In other words, they are most likely to view society in terms of our elite/mass (Type A), pyramid (Type B), or lower-middle (Type C) profiles. In contrast, those at the top of society, or those well off in terms of quality of life, careers, schooling, and opportunities, are more likely to view society as predominantly upper-middle class or egalitarian. These characterizations correspond, respectively, to our upper-middle (Type E) and middle profiles (Type D).

These propositions are tested in Tables 7 to 12. Shown in Tables 7 to 11 are standardized multiple regression coefficients of each of the five inequality profiles on eight socio-economic variables within each of 10 countries, as well as their total.[3] The two hierarchical class and status variables are education (measured in years of schooling)[4] and subjective social class employed in Table 1. A second-order hierarchical measure, which builds on these, is upward and downward mobility in terms of jobs, income, and education. Respondents were asked whether the status of their present job was higher, about equal, or lower than their father's;[5] whether their "income or standard of living" is better, about equal, or worse than their father's;[6] and whether they are better or worse off in education and training than their father when he was the same age as the respondent.[7] Thus, these three variables measure the degree of upward mobility experienced by respondents in three different areas. Gender and age were included as two ascriptive variables; that is, being in the realm of sociobiology, people have very little control over their placement in sex/gender and age categories, though transvestism suggests that sex/gender is less biologically rooted than age. They fall under the rubric of sex/gender and age stratification. Our expectation is that women and older persons will more likely choose the elite/mass pyramid and lower-middle profiles than the middle or upper-middle models. Age is curvilinear, with the greatest opportunities and status held by those in the middle of their working careers. Lastly, labour force participation is considered in all societies as an avenue to scarce resources in society. Those excluded from participating in jobs and associated income are more likely to be the dispossessed, and are likely to view society more in terms of deep divisions of inequality. Accordingly, a series of labour force participation dummy variables was constructed. The unemployed, students, housewives, retired, and other labour force nonparticipants were converted into 1/0 dummy variables, with labour force participants the excluded category.

These eight socio-economic variables have a small influence on the selection of the five profiles by respondents in ten of the countries in the 1992 ISSP surveys (Tables 7 to 11). The largest multiple correlation is .28 (elite/mass in New Zealand, Table 7). This only amounts to 8% of the variance explained in the choice of this profile over the others. In general, the socio-economic variables have somewhat greater effects on the selection of the elite/mass model in Table 7 than the others in Tables 8 to 11. But this is not the case for all countries, especially Hungary, the Czech Republic, and Poland, where the selection of the egalitarian middle profile seems as much affected as the elite/mass model by socio-economic background factors. The two hierarchical variables of education and subjective social class have the strongest and most negative effects on the selection of the elite/mass model, as expected. Those with the least education, placing themselves subjectively in the lower classes of society, are most likely to select this model of inequality, other background variables being held constant. This is particularly noteworthy in Bulgaria, Poland, and the Czech Republic (for class), Norway (for education), and Canada, New Zealand and Australia (for class and education). In contrast, education and subjective class have positive effects on the selection of the egalitarian middle-class model in Table 10. In other words, those with greater education, placing themselves in the upper-class categories, are more likely to select this egalitarian model, again independent of other background factors. As expected, those with lower education and subjective class placements, especially in Norway and Australia (for education), are also somewhat likely to select the pyramid model (Table 8). But these effects are considerably weaker than for the elite/mass model. Surprising is some preference by those of higher schooling and classes for the lower-middle in Table 9, especially in New Zealand and Australia. Perhaps this reflects the lower background from which the higher status holders rose, or the fear that those with higher status may one day fall into a larger lower-middle. Equally surprising is the choice of the upper-middle by low status-holders in Table 11. Only among higher social classes in Poland does there seem to be a leaning in this direction. In the Czech Republic, Italy, Australia, and the Philippines, there is a slight tendency for those with less schooling and in lower classes to select this model of society.

TABLE 7: STANDARDIZED REGRESSION COEFFICIENTS OF PERCEPTION
OF ELITE/MASS SOCIAL STRUCTURE TODAY (TYPE A)
ON SOCIO-ECONOMIC VARIABLES, BY COUNTRY

Country	Education (Yrs)	Subjective Class	Inter-Generational Mobility			Gender	Age	Labour Force Non-Participation					Summary		(n)
			Job	Income	Education			Unemployed	Student	Housewife	Retired	Other Non-Labour Force	R	r^2	
Hungary	.06	-.08*	.01	-.06	.05	-.01	—	-.03	.01	-.03	-.01	.00	.12	.02	1090
Czech Rep.	-.01	-.08*	-.01	.00	.01	.02	.01	-.02	-.02	-.01	-.01	.07*	.12	.01	1010
Poland	.01	-.09*	.04	-.05	.01	.02	.05	-.05	-.03	-.06	-.06	-.01	.13*	.02*	1245
Bulgaria	-.03	-.14*	.04	-.05	.02	-.02	.12*	.03	-.02	-.02	-.02	.04	.21*	.05*	941
Italy	-.05	-.12*	.12*	-.08	.04	.01	-.03	.04	.03	.01	.00	.08*	.19*	.04*	786
Norway	-.15*	-.05	.00	.00	.00	.05	-.04	.11*	-.07*	.00	-.02	-.04	.23*	.05*	1273
Canada	-.14*	-.11*	.08*	-.06	-.05	.04	.04	.04	-.02	.06	-.06	.00	.26*	.07*	874
New Zealand	-.08*	-.16*	.08*	-.14*	.01	.05	-.01	.02	-.02	.02	.04	-.03	.28*	.08*	1126
Australia	-.13*	-.13*	.06*	-.06*	.02	.06*	-.02	.06*	.00	.00	.04	.00	.23*	.05*	1763
Philippines	.07*	.00	-.04	.03	.02	-.05	.09*	.04	.02	.00	-.03	.01	.12	.02	1082
All	-.05*	-.20*	.08*	-.11*	.01	.03*	-.03*	.03*	-.04*	-.03*	.03*	.01	.27*	.07*	10163

Significance: T and F-tests: * p < .05

TABLE 8: STANDARDIZED REGRESSION COEFFICIENTS OF PERCEPTION
OF PYRAMID SOCIAL STRUCTURE TODAY (TYPE B)
ON SOCIO-ECONOMIC VARIABLES, BY COUNTRY

| Country | Education (Yrs) | Subjective Class | Inter-Generational Mobility | | | Gender | Age | Labour Force Non-Participation | | | | | Summary | | (n) |
			Job	Income	Education			Unemployed	Student	Housewife	Retired	Other Non-Labour Force	R	r^2	
Hungary	-.01	.02	.01	.03	-.01	.00	.03	.03	-.04	.05	-.02	.03	.10	.01	1090
Czech Rep.	.00	-.04	.02	-.01	.02	.00	.04	-.02	.08*	.00	.00	-.07*	.11	.01	1010
Poland	.07*	.03	-.02	.05	-.01	-.03	.03	-.01	.01	.08*	-.01	.03	.12	.01	1245
Bulgaria	.01	.06	-.05	.01	.03	.02	-.02	-.03	-.04	-.01	-.04	-.06	.12	.02	941
Italy	.00	.01	-.09*	.04	.03	-.07	.06	-.02	.04	.05	.02	-.04	.12	.02	786
Norway	-.12*	.03	.03	-.02	-.03	.06*	.03	-.04	.02	.00	.01	-.01	.21*	.04*	1273
Canada	-.02	.01	.01	.02	-.01	.01	.06	-.02	.00	.02	-.01	—	.07	.01	925
New Zealand	-.02	-.05	-.01	.12*	-.04	.02	.08	.00	.05	-.01	.02	.01	.15*	.02*	1126
Australia	-.11*	-.04	.05	.02	-.01	.01	.08*	-.02	.03	.03	.01	.00	.18*	.03*	1763
Philippines	.04	.06*	.00	-.04	-.05	.00	.01	-.03	-.01	.04	-.03	.02	.12	.01	1082
All	-.01	.01	.01	.02	-.01	.01	.06*	-.02	.00	.02*	-.01	.00	.07*	.01*	10163

Significance: T and F-tests: * p < .05

TABLE 9: STANDARDIZED REGRESSION COEFFICIENTS OF PERCEPTION OF LOWER-MIDDLE SOCIAL STRUCTURE TODAY (TYPE C) ON SOCIO-ECONOMIC VARIABLES, BY COUNTRY

Country	Education (Yrs)	Subjective Class	Inter-Generational Mobility			Gender	Age	Unemployed	Labour Force Non-Participation				Summary		(n)
			Job	Income	Education				Student	Housewife	Retired	Other Non-Labour Force	R	r²	
Hungary	-.06	.04	-.06	.04	-.02	-.01	-.04	-.01	.06*	-.02	.02	-.02	.12	.02	1090
Czech Rep.	-.01	.01	.02	-.03	.02	-.02	-.04	-.01	-.04	-.01	-.02	.03	.06	.00	1010
Poland	.04	.06	-.02	.02	-.01	.00	-.02	.04	.01	.02	.05	.00	.09	.01	1245
Bulgaria	.02	.04	-.01	.02	-.05	.02	-.07	-.02	.08*	.04	.04	.03	.14	.02	941
Italy	.03	.03	—	.00	-.08*	.02	-.09	-.04	-.09*	-.05	.04	-.06	.14	.02	786
Norway	.09*	.01	.00	-.01	.02	-.05	.08*	.00	.02	-.02	.00	.04	.13*	.02*	1273
Canada	-.02	.01	.01	.02	-.01	.01	.06	-.02	.00	.02	-.01	—	.07	.00	925
New Zealand	.09*	.15*	-.06	.02	.06	-.06	-.08*	—	-.02	—	-.04	.02	.26*	.06*	1126
Australia	.09*	.06*	-.04	-.02	-.03	-.06*	-.08*	-.03	-.01	.06*	-.02	.01	.18*	.03*	1763
Philippines	-.10*	-.01	.04	-.02	.06	.03	-.06	.01	.00	.00	.07*	-.03	.13	.02	1082
All	.04*	.12*	-.06*	.03*	.02	-.04*	.00	-.02	.00	—	-.02	.00	.16*	.03*	10163

Significance: T and F-tests: * p < .05

TABLE 10: STANDARDIZED REGRESSION COEFFICIENTS OF PERCEPTION OF MIDDLE SOCIAL STRUCTURE TODAY (TYPE D) ON SOCIO-ECONOMIC VARIABLES, BY COUNTRY

Country	Education (Yrs)	Subjective Class	Inter-Generational Mobility			Gender	Age	Labour Force Non-Participation					Summary		(n)
			Job	Income	Education			Unemployed	Student	Housewife	Retired	Other Non-Labour Force	R	r²	
Hungary	.00	.09*	.03	.04	-.07*	.04	.02	.01	.01	.00	.03	-.02	.14	.02	1090
Czech Rep.	.05	.12*	-.01	.04	-.06	-.01	-.01	.03	-.03	.03	.02	-.01	.16*	.02*	1010
Poland	-.08*	.00	—	.02	.02	.01	-.08	.06*	.04	-.05	.03	-.04	.13	.02	1245
Bulgaria	-.02	.10*	.02	.03	-.02	-.02	-.09	-.02	.03	.00	.04	.00	.15*	.02*	941
Italy	.05	.06	-.04	.02	-.01	.04	.03	.05	.00	.01	-.06	.03	.13	.02	786
Norway	.09*	.10*	-.03	.03	.01	-.02	-.07	-.03	.00	.02	.00	.00	.19*	.04*	1273
Canada	.05	.12*	-.02	.05	.02	-.05	-.08	.07*	.03	-.02	.03	.02	.20*	.04*	874
New Zealand	.03	.08*	-.02	-.01	-.02	-.03	-.04	-.04	-.02	-.04	.00	-.01	.13	.02	1126
Australia	.13*	.10*	-.06*	.05	.03	.01	.02	.00	-.02	-.03	-.02	-.01	.20*	.04*	1763
Philippines	.02	.00	-.05	.02	-.02	.06	-.06	-.02	-.01	.00	.02	.02	.10	.01	1082
All	.07*	.13*	-.06*	.08*	-.01	.00	-.01	.00	.04	.00	—	-.01	.20*	.04*	10163

Significance: T and F-tests: * p < .05

TABLE 11: STANDARDIZED REGRESSION COEFFICIENTS OF PERCEPTION OF UPPER-MIDDLE SOCIAL STRUCTURE TODAY (TYPE E) ON SOCIO-ECONOMIC VARIABLES, BY COUNTRY

Country	Education (Yrs)	Subjective Class	Inter-Generational Mobility			Gender	Age	Labour Force Non-Participation					Summary		(n)
			Job	Income	Education			Unemployed	Student	Housewife	Retired	Other Non-Labour Force	R	r²	
Hungary	-.07	-.04	-.03	-.03	.02	-.03	-.06	.01	-.02	-.02	.00	-.01	.11	.01	1090
Czech Rep.	-.09*	.00	-.07	.01	.02	-.03	-.03	.07*	-.03	-.02	-.03	-.02	.15*	.02*	1010
Poland	-.09*	.10*	-.01	-.04	-.02	.00	-.05	.01	-.04	.02	.07	.01	.14*	.02*	1245
Bulgaria	.01	.01	-.02	.05	-.05	.00	-.03	.06	-.03	.06	.02	-.02	.11	.01	941
Italy	-.07	-.01	.06	.00	.03	.03	.03	-.01	.01	-.04	.01	.03	.12	.01	786
Norway	.00	.00	.03	.01	-.02	-.01	-.03	.03	.02	.01	.01	-.02	.06	.00	1273
Canada	.01	-.05	.05	-.06	-.06	.05	.08	-.02	.04	-.02	.09*	.01	.19*	.03*	874
New Zealand	-.04	.01	.04	-.03	.01	.04	.12*	.06	.02	.06	-.10*	—	.15*	.02*	1126
Australia	-.02	-.08*	.01	-.01	-.04	-.04	-.02	-.02	-.02	-.01	.01	.02	.10	.01	1763
Philippines	-.12*	-.10*	.07*	.00	-.01	-.01	-.04	-.01	.00	-.06	.00	-.04	.18*	.03*	1082
All	-.07*	-.03*	.02*	-.01	-.02	-.01	-.03*	.01	—	.01	.00	-.01	.09*	.01*	10163

Significance: T and F-tests: * p < .05

One expects that the upwardly mobile would identify with egalitarian or upper-middle class models of society, and the downwardly mobile with models of inequality, especially of the elite/mass nature. This expectation is mostly borne out only in the case of income mobility in the elite/mass model of Table 7: respondents, especially in New Zealand, who feel they are much worse off than their fathers in terms of their income and standard of living are somewhat more likely to select this model of inequality. But there is no pronounced tendency for the upwardly mobile to select the more egalitarian models, independent of other background factors.

Are women more likely than men to characterize society in terms of deep divisions of social inequality? Most of the gender coefficients in Tables 7 to 11 are small and statistically non-significant at the .05 level (women were coded "1," men "0"). There is some evidence in Table 7 that women are more likely to choose the elite/mass model in Norway, Canada, New Zealand, and Australia, and the pyramid model in Norway in Table 8. Men seem slightly more likely than women to choose the lower-middle and middle-class models in Tables 9 and 10, respectively.

Older persons and those excluded from labour force participation are also expected to select inegalitarian over egalitarian models of society. This is somewhat borne out in Table 7, where older Bulgarians appear to choose the elite/mass model. The unemployed in Norway and Australia also seem to have some preference for this model. Polish housewives have some preference for the pyramid model in Table 8, perhaps reflecting their generally low position in society. On the other hand, the younger appear to favour slightly the egalitarian middle-class profile in Table 10. Yet there are exceptions to these statements, such as the slight tendency for the unemployed in Poland and Canada to choose the middle-class profile. In general, though, none of these effects are strong. We will return to this question with a possible explanation in the section on the Dispossessed.

In Table 1 at the beginning of the chapter, we found evidence of strong subjective class differences between countries. It is therefore reasonable to suppose that the influences of socio-economic status and class variables on the five profiles are confounded with differences between countries. A legitimate question is whether national social and political culture influence the selection of egalitarian versus inegalitarian models of society independent of the background socio-economic variables we have just been considering.

Evidence bearing on this question is presented in Table 12. Deleting education[8] and intergenerational mobility, country dummy variables are introduced (Canada is the excluded category). The effect is to raise considerably the variance explained in each of the five profile variables over levels attained in Tables 7 to 11. This results from inter-country differences in the choice of inequality profiles. Independent of class, gender, age, and labour force participation, citizens in the less developed countries of Hungary, Poland, Bulgaria, and the Philippines are much more likely to select the unequal elite/mass profile of society than are residents in Canada, Italy, Norway, New Zealand, and Australia. The Czech Republic may be the one exception to this strong pattern. The country and socio-economic variables together explain 17% of the variance in selecting the elite/mass model over the others (R = .41). In contrast, the Eastern European countries and the Philippines are much less likely to select the other models of society. The upper classes (b = .09) and the Norwegians (b = .22) have a particular preference for the middle-class model. The upper-middle-class model is the least affected by differences in national culture; along with the middle-class profile, it is the one model morally preferred by many countries.

CONFLICT AND FRAGMENTATION

So far we have discussed and analyzed social structures of inequality and attitudes toward these structures. A long-standing question in the social sciences has been the influence of social structure on people's capacity to act in terms of one or more divisions, such as class, gender, age, and rural/urban differences. One answer to this question lies in the capacity or willingness to view social conflict in society as a result of group interests and as an initial step to, or ingredient of, social and political action. The images one has of the system of social inequality is expected to influence whether or not one sees the potential for conflict in society, or the particular nature of such conflict. More specifically, it has long been argued that the privileged in society have an interest in maintaining order and stability, and avoiding conflict, at least the kind that might challenge their position of relative power and affluence. By the same token, it has been argued that the less privileged have an interest in any conflict that poses a challenge to the more privileged, because such a challenge might improve their own group or individual position in society. In light of these considerations, we hypothesize that those of lower socio-economic

TABLE 12: REGRESSION OF FIVE INEQUALITY PROFILES ON COUNTRIES AND SOCIO-ECONOMIC VARIABLES, 1992

Inequality Profiles:

Socio-economic variables and country	Elite/ Mass	Pyramid Middle	Lower Middle	Middle	Upper Middle
Subjective Class	-.10*	-.01	.06*	.09*	-.04*
Gender	.02	.01	-.03*	—	-.01
Age	.02	.05*	-.05*	-.04*	.00
Out of Labour Force					
retired	-.01	.00	.00	.00	.01
unemployed	.02	-.01	-.02	.00	.02
housewife	-.01	.02	-.01	.00	-.01
student	-.01	.02	-.01	.01	.00
other non-labour force	.01	-.01	.00	.00	.00
Country Dummy Variable (Canada Excluded Category)					
Hungary	.16*	-.02	-.10*	-.07*	-.01
Czech Republic	.03*	.02	-.06*	.00	-.01
Poland	.24*	-.10*	-.11*	-.06*	.01
Bulgaria	.20*	-.07*	-.09*	-.05*	-.04*
Italy	-.04*	-.02	.00	.03*	.08*
Norway	-.07*	-.13*	.02	.22*	-.01
New Zealand	.03*	.02	.01	-.06*	-.03*
Australia	-.04*	-.03*	.06*	.04*	-.04*
Philippines	.13*	-.05*	-.08*	-.05*	.07*
R	.41*	.17*	.24*	.32*	.14*
R^2	.17*	.03*	.06*	.10*	.02*
(n)	11409	11409	11409	11409	11409

Significance: F- and t-tests: * $p < .05$.

status, as well as those who view society as more deeply divided by social inequalities (such as the elite/mass model), will see a much greater potential for social conflict on a number of bases than those of higher status and class and those who hold more egalitarian or upper-middle-class views.

Six bases of conflict will be considered: 1) rich versus poor; 2) working versus middle classes; 3) the unemployed versus the employed;

4) management versus workers; 5) farmers versus city folk; and 6) young versus older people. Respondents in the ISSP surveys were asked, "In all countries, there are differences or even conflicts between different social groups. In your opinion, in [your country], how much conflict is there between ..." This was followed by four choices for each of the above six bases of conflict recoded as: "very strong conflicts" 4), "strong conflicts" 3), "not very strong conflicts" 2), and "there are no conflicts" 1). The six were averaged into an overall conflict index. Because the nature and origins of the six dimensions of conflict may be quite different, we examine them separately, as well as together in the conflict index, in Tables 13 to 19. They are regressed onto the four inequality profiles, as well as onto the socio-economic background variables we have been considering thus far. Our hypothesis is that respondents in the 10 countries who subscribe especially to the elite/mass profile, and who come from lower social origins, will more likely see the potential for conflict in society in terms of class, wealth and income, age, and region. Because different kinds of conflict do not have the same social bases, we introduced a rural/urban community size variable in studying the conflict between farmers and city folk (Table 17).[9] Trade union membership has been introduced in recognition of its possible relevance for conflict between management and workers, as well as between the working and middle classes, and the rich and poor.[10] We have purposely used age and retirement earlier in the chapter in anticipation of their possible relevance for the conflict between younger and older people (Table 18).

Education and subjective social class have generally negative effects on all types of social conflict. The strongest is the negative effect in Table 13 of education on perception of the conflict between the rich and poor in Canada (b = -.23). The main exception to these negative effects is Bulgaria, where education and class appear to have positive effects on all six types of conflict. Turning to intergenerational mobility, one expects the downwardly mobile more than the upwardly mobile to see greater conflict in society. Mobility in terms of jobs, income, and education generally have negative effects on conflict. This suggests that the downwardly mobile are the most likely to view social divisions in terms of conflict. This is particularly the case for income mobility which, for example, has particularly negative effects on perceptions of conflict between management and workers in Poland (b = -.10) and Canada (b = -.13) (Table 16). However, these influences are weak, and there are some instances in which the upwardly mobile view a greater potential for conflict in society. This is

TABLE 13: STANDARDIZED REGRESSION COEFFICIENTS OF PERCEPTION OF CONFLICT BETWEEN THE RICH AND POOR ON SOCIO-ECONOMIC VARIABLES, BY COUNTRY

Country	Education (Yrs)	Inter-Generational Mobility				Gender	Age	Labour Force Non-Participation					Trade Union Membership	Social Structure				Summary		(n)
		Subjective Class	Job	Income	Education			Unemployed	Student	Housewife	Retired	Other Non-Labour Force		Elite/Mass	Pyramid	Lower Middle	Upper Middle	R	r^2	
Hungary	-.01	-.03	-.02	-.05	.01	.01	.11*	-.03	-.03	-.04	-.06	.00	-.04	.20*	.16*	.02	.10*	.20*	.04*	1088
Czech Rep.	-.06	.06	-.03	.01	-.08*	.05	-.09	-.02	.00	.05	.12*	.01	-.03	.16*	.07	.03	.13*	.26*	.07*	838
Poland	-.10*	.01	.01	-.06	.01	.04	-.03	.00	-.02	-.06	.06	.02	.00	.02	.04	-.05	-.04	.17*	.03*	1223
Bulgaria	.03	.03	.06	-.06	—	.08*	.06	—	-.03	—	-.07*	.01	-.14*	.06	-.04	-.01	.02	.18*	.03*	894
Italy	-.06	-.05	-.05	.02	.07	.03	-.03	-.01	.01	.05	.01	.08*	@	.10*	.06	-.02	.06	.20*	.04*	780
Norway	-.10*	-.16*	.04	-.02	.01	.10*	-.08*	.05	.05	.00	.11*	.04	.02	.09*	.09*	.06*	.02	.32*	.10*	1273
Canada	-.23*	-.06	-.02	-.03	.02	.13*	.01	.00	-.04	-.02	-.05	.00	.02	.10*	.08	-.02	.11*	.35*	.12*	702
New Zealand	-.02	-.09*	-.02	-.04	.03	.08*	-.01	.04	-.04	.01	-.08*	-.02	@	.25*	.13*	.02	.08*	.31*	.10*	1126
Australia	-.13*	-.08*	.04	-.06*	.02	.04	-.09*	.00	.02	.02	.03	.00	.05*	.19*	.16*	.05	.02	.30*	.09*	1763
Philippines	.03	.00	-.06	.02	-.02	.00	.01	—	.01	-.01	-.02	-.01	@	.01	-.02	-.01	-.04	.08	.01	1082
All	-.07*	-.06*	.01	-.05*	.02	.05*	-.03*	.00	-.01	.01	.02	.02	-.03*	.20*	.14*	.07*	.03*	.25*	.06*	9481

Significance: T and F-tests: * $p < .05$
@ Excluded from analysis because of small numbers.

TABLE 14: STANDARDIZED REGRESSION COEFFICIENTS OF PERCEPTION
OF CONFLICT BETWEEN THE WORKING AND MIDDLE CLASSES
ON SOCIO-ECONOMIC VARIABLES, BY COUNTRY

Country	Education (Yrs)	Inter-Generational Mobility						Labour Force Non-Participation						Social Structure				Summary		
		Subjective Class	Job	Income	Education	Gender	Age	Unemployed	Student	Housewife	Retired	Other Non-Labour Force	Trade Union Membership	Elite/Mass	Pyramid	Lower Middle	Upper Middle	R	r²	(n)
Hungary	-.09*	-.03	-.07	.00	.06	.02	.04	.00	-.04	-.01	.01	.05	-.03	.06	.04	.00	.09*	.20*	.04*	1088
Czech Rep.	-.05	.05	-.05	.02	-.06	.01	-.05	.00	.01	.00	.09*	.01	.01	.10*	.06	.06	.11*	.17	.03	904
Poland	-.08*	.07*	-.05	-.05	.00	.02	-.07	—	-.04	-.02	.10*	.05	.03	-.01	.04	-.09	.03	.17*	.03*	1239
Bulgaria	.04	.01	.04	-.09*	.03	.07*	.05*	-.04	.00	.00	-.08	-.06	-.12*	.01	.00	.05	.00	.15	.02	860
Italy	-.05	-.06	.01	.01	.05	.07	-.09	.03	-.01	.05	.07	.04	@	.05	.03	-.05	.00	.18*	.03*	775
Norway	-.08*	-.12*	.04	—	-.03	.08*	-.05	.01	-.01	-.01	.03	.02	-.02	.08*	.09*	.06*	.06*	.25*	.06*	1273
Canada	-.08	-.02	.08	-.09*	-.04	.07	.01	-.01	-.01	.03	-.04	.06	-.02	.07	.02	.03	.10*	.22*	.05*	702
New Zealand	-.06*	-.04	.04	-.06	-.01	.07*	.02	.00	-.04	.02	-.12*	-.02	@	.17*	.10*	.04	.03	.24*	.06*	1116
Australia	-.07*	-.05*	.03	-.04	.00	.04	-.06*	.04	.05*	.02	.04	.01	.03	.16*	.13*	-.01	.02	.25*	.06*	1763
Philippines	.00	.01	.04	.04	-.06	-.01	.01	-.02	.04	.02	-.05	.03	@	-.06	-.09	-.04	-.04	.12	.01	1082
All	-.10*	-.03*	.03*	-.04*	-.01	.03*	-.04*	-.01	-.01	.04*	.00	.01	-.03*	.11*	.09*	.02	.08*	.20*	.04*	9481

Significance: T and F-tests: * p < .05
@ Excluded from analysis because of small numbers.

TABLE 15: STANDARDIZED REGRESSION COEFFICIENTS OF PERCEPTION OF CONFLICT BETWEEN THE UNEMPLOYED AND EMPLOYED ON SOCIO-ECONOMIC VARIABLES, BY COUNTRY

Country	Education (Yrs)	Subjective Class	Inter-Generational Mobility			Gender	Age	Labour Force Non-Participation						Social Structure				Summary		
			Job	Income	Education			Unemployed	Student	Housewife	Retired	Other Non-Labour Force	Trade Union Membership	Elite/Mass	Pyramid	Lower Middle	Upper Middle	R	r²	(n)
Hungary	-.01	.01	.04	-.03	-.02	.03	.06	-.02	-.05	.01	.04	.11*	.01	-.04	-.02	—	.01	.18*	.03*	1088
Czech Rep.	-.04	.01	-.07	.01	.04	.12*	.02	.03	.00	.07*	.11*	.03	.00	.18*	.04	.05	.10*	.27*	.07*	904
Poland	-.15*	.08*	.03	-.06	.01	.10*	-.08	.01	-.03	-.02	.12*	.02	.02	.02	.04	.02	.00	.20*	.04*	1208
Bulgaria	.08	.06	.02	-.04	.02	.07*	.10	.02	-.03	.03	-.05	-.02	-.10*	-.01	-.01	-.03	-.02	.16	.02	890
Italy	-.03	-.04	-.06	.04	.11*	.09*	.04	-.02	.04	.05	-.02	.03	@	.07	-.02	-.04	.03	.21*	.04*	777
Norway	-.04	-.10*	.02	-.02	.01	.18*	-.13*	.02	.03	.01	.09*	.01	-.02	.11*	.06*	.06*	.03*	.29*	.08*	1273
Canada	-.11*	-.06	-.01	.00	-.02	.12*	-.05	.01	-.03	.01	.00	.02	.06	.07	.06	.01	.10*	.26*	.07*	702
New Zealand	-.06*	—	-.03	-.02	.05	.08*	-.06	.00	-.02	.04	-.07	.02	@	.18*	.07	.02	.06	.25*	.06*	1116
Australia	-.07*	-.06*	.00	-.03	.04	.10*	-.08*	.02	.01	.05*	.02	-.02	.06*	.16*	.14*	.03	.05*	.27*	.07*	1763
Philippines	.04	.00	.03	-.02	—	.08*	.05	.02	.02	-.04	-.03	—	@	-.01	-.01	.01	.00	.10	.01	1082
All	-.05*	.00	.00	-.02	.03*	.09*	-.01	.01	.00	.04*	.02	.03*	—	.09*	.07*	.03*	.05*	.15*	.02*	9481

Significance: T and F-tests: * p < .05
@ Excluded from analysis because of small numbers.

TABLE 16: STANDARDIZED REGRESSION COEFFICIENTS OF PERCEPTION
OF CONFLICT BETWEEN MANAGEMENT AND WORKERS
ON SOCIO-ECONOMIC VARIABLES, BY COUNTRY

Country	Education (Yrs)	Subjective Class	Inter-Generational Mobility			Gender	Age	Unemployed	Student	Housewife	Retired	Other Non-Labour Force	Trade Union Membership	Social Structure				Summary		(n)
			Job	Income	Education									Elite/Mass	Pyramid	Lower Middle	Upper Middle	R	r²	
Hungary	-.01	-.08*	-.02	-.03	.00	-.02	-.06	.01	-.01	-.05	-.02	.05	-.08*	.06	-.01	-.02	.04	.20*	.04*	1088
Czech Rep.	-.04	.00	-.07	-.01	.01	.02	-.10*	.02	.06	-.01	.04	-.01	.01	.14*	.05	.00	.10*	.21*	.04*	917
Poland	-.03	.00	.06	-.10*	.00	.03	-.14*	.02	.01	.02	.13*	.05	-.01	.09	.06	.04	.06	.16*	.03*	1210
Bulgaria	.08	.01	-.02	-.04	—	-.03	-.04	-.03	-.03	.01	-.02	-.05	-.02	.03	-.02	.04	-.04	.14	.02	895
Italy	-.06	.00	.01	-.01	.03	.06	-.06	-.04	-.01	-.02	-.03	.04	@	.06	.04	-.05	.06	.16	.02	771
Norway	-.03	-.14*	-.04	.01	.00	.03	-.14*	.01	.06	-.01	.01	.01	.03	.11*	.02	.09*	-.05	.27*	.07*	1273
Canada	-.04	-.06	.08	-.13*	.06	-.02	.01	.04	—	.06	-.04	—	.04	.00	.03	.02	.07	.19	.04	702
New Zealand	-.03	-.09*	-.02	.00	.04	.06	-.07	.02	.01	.01	-.08*	-.06	@	.12*	.12*	.05	.06*	.22*	.05*	1125
Australia	-.06*	-.07*	.01	-.04	.05	.02	-.09*	.01	.05*	.00	.03	.00	.12*	.14*	.10*	.03	.05*	.25*	.06*	1763
Philippines	.03	.01	-.05	-.01	-.07*	.01	-.02	-.02	-.02	.00	.04	.04	@	-.02	-.06	-.01	-.01	.12	.01	1082
All	-.03*	-.04*	.00	-.05*	.02*	.02	-.07*	.00	—	.00	—	.02	.02	.13*	.09*	.04*	.06*	.16*	.02*	9481

Significance: T and F-tests: * p < .05
@ Excluded from analysis because of small numbers.

TABLE 17: STANDARDIZED REGRESSION COEFFICIENTS OF PERCEPTION OF CONFLICT BETWEEN FARMERS AND CITY PEOPLE ON SOCIO-ECONOMIC VARIABLES, BY COUNTRY

Country	Education (Yrs)	Inter-Generational Mobility				Gender	Age	Labour Force Non-Participation							Social Structure				Summary		
		Subjective Class	Job	Income	Education			Unemployed	Student	Housewife	Retired	Other Non-Labour Force	Trade Union Membership	Community Size	Elite/Mass	Pyramid	Lower Middle	Upper Middle	R	r²	(n)
Hungary	-.02	.06	-.04	.00	.02	.01	-.08	-.05	-.03	.06	.06	.11*	-.03	-.08*	.04	.07	.01	.05	.18*	.03*	1088
Czech Rep.	.00	.04	-.04	.01	-.02	.01	-.05	.00	.04	.06	.08	.01	@	-.12*	.09*	.03	.07	.12*	.23*	.05*	876
Poland	-.01	.04	.01	-.02	.02	.10*	—	.00	-.01	-.06*	.05	-.02	-.06	-.03	.02	.04	.01	.02	.15	.02	1241
Bulgaria	.02	—	-.01	-.04	.02	.04	-.07	-.05	.05	.02	.01	-.06	-.08*	.08*	—	.00	.02	.00	.17	.03	873
Italy	-.09*	.01	—	-.03	.04	-.02	.01	-.04	.03	.00	-.08	.11*	@	-.06	.01	.01	-.10*	.03	.21*	.04*	758
Norway	.04	-.06	.00	-.04	.06*	-.03	-.10*	.03	.03	-.01	.03	.07*	-.01	-.03	.13*	.07*	.05	-.01	.22*	.05*	1273
Canada	-.09*	-.07	.05	.01	-.07	.10*	-.10*	.02	.01	-.01	-.02	.08*	-.04	-.11*	.03	.03	.04	.09*	.26*	.07*	702
New Zealand	-.07*	-.07*	.01	.02	.01	.07*	-.02	.01	.00	.01	-.06	-.02	@	-.05	.08	.04	-.02	.00	.20*	.04*	1124
Australia	-.06*	-.01	.00	-.06*	.06*	.09*	-.08*	.02	.05*	-.06*	.03	.00	.08*	-.07*	.15*	.11*	.04	.06*	.26*	.07*	1763
Philippines	-.02	-.01	.00	—	-.05	.08*	-.02	.01	.02	-.03	.01	—	@	@	.01	-.02	—	.02	.11	.01	1082
All	-.06*	.04*	-.01	-.01	.02	.04*	-.02	-.01	.03	.02	-.02	.02	-.03	.01	.04	.03	.01	.03	.11*	.01*	3770

Significance: T and F-tests: * p < .05

@ Excluded from analysis because of small numbers.

Wording and code varies by country. Rural/urban in general sample; community size in specific countries.

TABLE 18: STANDARDIZED REGRESSION COEFFICIENTS OF PERCEPTION
OF CONFLICT BETWEEN YOUNG AND OLDER PEOPLE
ON SOCIO-ECONOMIC VARIABLES, BY COUNTRY

Country	Education (Yrs)	Subjective Class	Job	Income	Education	Gender	Age	Unemployed	Student	Housewife	Retired	Other Non-Labour Force	Trade Union Member	Elite/Mass	Pyramid	Lower Middle	Upper Middle	R	r^2	(n)
		Inter-Generational Mobility						Labour Force Non-Participation						Social Structure				Summary		
Hungary	.05	.01	-.04	-.02	.02	.04	.08	-.03	.02	.00	.02	.06	-.09*	-.14*	-.14*	-.04	-.03	.17*	.03*	1088
Czech Rep.	-.02	.03	-.06	-.01	.01	.05	.05	-.04	.15*	-.02	.06	-.02	.01	.06	.00	-.01	.11*	.23*	.05*	914
Poland	.02	.05	.03	-.04	-.02	.07*	-.07	.02	.00	.00	.14*	.10*	-.02	.03	.03	.01	.00	.17*	.03*	1245
Bulgaria	.12*	.03	-.06	.02	-.02	.11*	-.04	-.07*	.05	-.03	—	-.01	-.06	-.06	-.07	-.02	-.06	.22*	.05*	898
Italy	-.05	.03	.02	.02	-.02	.06	-.03	-.05	.04	-.01	.03	.06	@	-.05	.04	-.11*	-.05	.16	.03	776
Norway	.07*	-.06	-.05	.01	-.01	.05	-.01	.09*	.13*	.00	.04	.04	-.02	.02	.06	.01	.00	.19*	.03*	1273
Canada	-.11*	-.08	.04	.05	-.02	.06	-.03	.06	.07	-.02	-.02	.04	-.04	.07	.06	—	.07	.23*	.05*	702
New Zealand	-.04	-.04	.06	-.01	.05	.05	-.02	.04	.00	.02	.00	.02	@	.11*	.06	-.02	.05	.18*	.03*	1126
Australia	-.05*	-.06*	.04	-.05*	.04	.10*	-.06*	.03	.00	.00	.04	.02	.04	.15*	.08*	.03	.03	.22*	.05*	1763
Philippines	.03	-.01	-.01	-.01	-.01	.03	.06	.04	—	.00	-.02	-.03	@	-.08	-.05	.01	.02	.11	.01	1082
All	-.01	-.01	.01	-.01	.02	.06*	.00	.00	.03*	—	.00	.03*	-.03*	.06*	.04*	.00	.03*	.11*	.01*	9481

Significance: T and F-tests: * p < .05
@ Excluded from analysis because of small numbers.

TABLE 19: STANDARDIZED REGRESSION COEFFICIENTS
OF CONFLICT INDEX
ON SOCIO-ECONOMIC VARIABLES, BY COUNTRY

Country	Education (Yrs)	Inter-Generational Mobility				Gender	Age	Labour Force Non-Participation						Social Structure				Summary		(n)
		Subjective Class	Job	Income	Education			Unemployed	Student	Housewife	Retired	Other Non-Labour Force	Trade Union Member	Elite/Mass	Pyramid	Lower Middle	Upper Middle	R	r^2	
Hungary	.03	-.02	-.04	-.04	.02	.02	.03	-.02	-.04	-.02	.02	.09*	-.07*	.03	.01	-.01	.06	.18*	.03*	1088
Czech Rep.	-.06	.01	-.06	.01	-.04	.09*	-.09	-.03	.07	.01	.12*	-.03	.00	.21*	.09	.03	.18*	.30*	.09*	620
Poland	-.08	.03	.04	-.07	-.02	.09*	-.09*	-.01	-.03	-.01	.15*	.06	-.03	.07	.09	.02	.05	.21*	.04*	887
Bulgaria	.11*	.04	-.01	-.05	.00	.07	.01	-.05	-.02	.02	-.06	-.05	-.11*	.01	-.04	.01	-.04	.18	.03	717
Italy	-.08*	-.03	-.02	.01	.08	-.04	-.04	-.02	.04	.04	.01	.07	@	.06	.02	-.09*	.04	.21*	.05*	736
Norway	-.04	-.14*	.04	.00	.01	.11*	-.12*	.06	.10*	—	.07*	.02	.02	.14*	.10*	.08*	.02	.31*	.10*	1162
Canada	-.17*	-.09*	.04	-.04	-.01	.12*	-.05	.02	-.01	-.01	-.04	.05	.01	.07	.07	.03	.14*	.32*	.10*	664
New Zealand	-.06	-.08*	.01	-.05	.03	.10*	-.04	.04	-.02	.03	-.11*	-.02	@	.22*	.12*	.01	.06	.32*	.11*	1041
Australia	-.10*	-.08*	.03	-.06*	.05	.10*	-.10*	.03	.05*	.04	.04	.00	.10*	.23*	.17*	.04	.06*	.35*	.12*	1763
Philippines	.03	-.01	-.01	-.01	-.05	.05	.04	.01	.02	-.02	-.02	.00	@	-.04	-.07	-.01	-.01	.10	.01	1082
All	-.07*	-.04*	.01	-.04*	.02	.07*	-.04*	-.01	.01	.03*	.00	.03*	-.02	.16*	.12*	.04*	.08*	.22*	.05*	8685

Significance: T and F-tests: * p < .05
@ Excluded from analysis because of small numbers.

particularly the case for Italy in Table 15 in the effect of educational mobility on the conflict between the employed and unemployed (b = .11).

Our hypothesis about sex/gender is that the disadvantaged sex (women) will see more conflict in society than men. This receives widespread support in Tables 13 to 19. In practically every country, and for each of the six conflict dimensions and in the overall conflict index, men are less likely to see society through the lens of conflict. This is especially so for the conflict between the unemployed and employed in Table 15. Women experience household-related aspects of unemployment not likely captured in official statistics and measures of labour force participation. In seeking jobs, their competition against the employed embraces not only the universal criteria used in hiring, but also explicit and implicit gender discrimination not experienced by men.

Age has small and contradictory effects on perceptions of conflict, though the most consistent appear negative, implying that young people are more likely to view society in terms of conflict. The wisdom of separating the effects of age from retirement is suggested in Poland, where, for example in Table 19, age has a negative effect (b = -.09), and retirement a positive effect (b = .15), on the conflict index. The forced exclusion from the labour force due to biology, advancing age, or law may predispose one to view society as more conflictual than the "natural" progression of age. Young persons, especially where job opportunities are not great, may be more likely to see society in terms of conflict between groups than mature and older workers with steady jobs. Perhaps surprisingly, with the exception of Poland, age and retirement do not seem to have substantially greater effects on perceptions of conflict between older and younger people in Table 18 than on the five other dimensions of conflict in Tables 13 to 17. The other categories of non-labour force participation (unemployed, students, housewives, and "other non-labour force") have small and contradictory effects on conflict. However, the largest effects appear positive, especially for the "other non-labour force" in the conflict between farmers and city people in Table 17 (note Hungary, Italy, Norway, and Canada). Students in Norway and the Czech Republic perceive more conflict between young and older persons than do labour force participants in Table 18. There is modest support for the proposition that exclusion from the labour force leads to a greater consciousness of a potential for conflict in society.

Much of the international literature on trade unions suggests that union members have somewhat higher levels of class consciousness, and often take more left positions on a variety of social and political issues. We therefore thought that this variable, independent of other influences, would contribute to viewing society in terms of conflict. A close examination of Tables 13 to 19 suggests an East/West or developed/underdeveloped country differentiation in this proposition. There is mild empirical support for the notion that trade union members in developed countries (especially Australia) are somewhat more likely to view society in terms of conflict; in less developed countries (the Philippines) and the former communist eastern bloc countries of Hungary, Bulgaria, Poland, and the Czech Republic, trade union members are significantly less likely to see society through the lens of conflict. This is not surprising given that trade union institutions were better integrated into established political and economic structures in the ex-communist bloc than in the West, despite notable exceptions like Mexico.

In Table 17, we introduce a special variable—community size—in examining the roots of the conflict between farmers and city people. Our assumption is that farmers and small town folks often feel powerless and alienated toward large metropolitan centres, the seats of political and economic power in most nations. They are thus more likely to view the relations between city and country in terms of conflict. The negative regression coefficients in Table 17 largely support this proposition, albeit not at a strong level. Especially in Hungary, the Czech Republic, Italy, Canada, and Australia, respondents in smaller communities are more likely to view their relations with larger urban centres in terms of conflict. This is independent of other influences considered in this table. The main exception appears to be Bulgaria, where urban dwellers think there is more conflict with farmers, independent of other factors.

The last, and perhaps most significant, set of variables in Tables 13 to 19 are the five inequality profiles in *today's society*. To be considered as independent variables, they were dummied into 1/0 scores, with the middle-class profile (Type D) the excluded category. The regression coefficients of the others are positive and negative variations around the middle-class profile. Compared to the egalitarian middle profile, those subscribing to one of the inequality profiles are more likely to view society in terms of conflict. This is especially so for those supporting the elite/mass image of society, particularly in the Czech Republic, Norway, New Zealand, and Australia. In order of influence on conflict, the elite/mass model ranks first, followed by the pyramid, upper-middle, and lower-middle models. The main exception to this pattern seems to be Italy, where residents who hold a middle-class view of society are significantly more likely to see the potential for conflict than those holding the lower-middle-class profile. Overall, the inequality profiles have much stronger effects than the socio-economic background variables on perceptions of conflict. This is particularly the case for the elite/mass and pyramid models.

In conclusion, the perception that society is split into conflicting groups with opposed interests is modestly rooted in lower *objective* structural positions of society, and the *subjective* perceptions that inequalities persist, especially between a small, rich, and powerful elite and a much larger mass of poor and powerless people at the bottom of society.

THE DISPOSSESSED

The dispossessed, the powerless, those at the bottom of society's hierarchical systems of inequality, whether in terms of income, education, occupational prestige, or power, are often disadvantaged in social science research. Surveys, interviews, questionnaires, and statistical analyses are class relations for such people. As clients they are confronted at the door, on the phone, or in the mails with representatives of research institutions of a higher social standing. They are thus not likely to be at ease in such social situations. In addition, the kinds of questions posed in social surveys have traditionally been devised by middle- and upper-middle-class persons with a greater grasp of complex theoretical and methodological issues than the lower-class persons being interviewed. Despite measures to overcome these obstacles, such biases often persist in social analyses.

In the ISSP surveys, considerable effort was exercised in trying to overcome some of these difficulties by employing the pictorial or graphic representations of the five inequality profiles used throughout this chapter. A legitimate question to ask is the extent to which such a strategy was able to elicit valid responses from those at the bottom of society. This question is of concern, since the structures of inequality lie at the heart of this chapter, and indeed the whole book. A supplementary question is whether the small effects of the non-labour force participant categories noted previously might have been attenuated by the inability of the least privileged in society to cope with the survey questions. In Tables 20 to 22, an attempt is made to analyze the "don't know" and "can't choose" responses to the profile questions, which so far in this chapter have been excluded from the analyses of data.

TABLE 20: PERCENT "CAN'T CHOOSE" OR "DON'T KNOW"ON SOCIAL
STRUCTURE INEQUALITY PROFILE QUESTIONS, BY COUNTRY *

Country	Historical Period			Morally Preferred Structure
	30 years ago	Now	30 years from now	
Hungary	23	8	32	10
Czech Republic	16	3	16	3
Poland	24	14	41	16
Bulgaria	24	16	35	17
Norway	6	4	14	4
Canada	8	6	10	6
New Zealand	3	2	7	3
Philippines	9	2	12	4

* In Italy and Australia, no respondents were coded as "can't choose" or
"don't know" on the social structure inequality profile questions.

In Table 20, the percentage of respondents in eight countries who replied "don't know" or "can't choose" when presented with the five inequality profiles is shown for the three time periods and the morally preferred structure. Three patterns are immediately evident. First, the respondents in the Eastern European countries displayed much greater difficulty with the inequality profile questions than those in the western developed countries and the Philippines. In some cases, the East's "non-response" is four times greater than the West's. For example, 35% of Bulgarians selected a "don't know" or "can't choose" when asked to select a profile 30 years into the future; this is more than four times higher than the 7% non-response in New Zealand. Second, in all countries respondents had more difficulty when asked to select a profile for 30 years ago, and for 30 years into the future, than for today's society. This is to be expected, since projection into the past relies considerably on memory and the willingness to fill in the blanks, and projection 30 years into the future takes on a hypothetical quality. Third, even by the standards of social science research, the levels of non-response are moderately high in some countries, reaching two-fifths of the sample for the selection of a future profile in Poland. Difficulties in coping with survey questions are not of concern if they are randomly distributed across socio-demographic characteristics of samples. They are of more concern where they are systematically related to the variables at the heart of a project, such as social inequality in this book. The relatively high proportion of "don't know" and "can't choose" responses could possibly be a reason for the relatively weak effects of several of the socio-economic background variables on the selection of the inequality profiles in this chapter.

In Tables 21 and 22, the influence of several of the socio-economic variables considered thus far in the chapter are shown, as is the influence of country. The cell figures are standardized multiple regression coefficients. The "don't know index" in the last column of Table 21, and in Table 22, is the summation of the "don't know" and "can't choose" responses to the five inequality profile questions across the three time periods and the morally preferred structure. These are regressed onto socio-economic factors and countries (as dummy variables) in Table 21. In Table 22, analyses of the socio-economic variables are carried out separately within each country.

TABLE 21: REGRESSION OF "DON'T KNOW" RESPONSES TO
SOCIAL STRUCTURE QUESTION ON SOCIO-ECONOMIC VARIABLES
AND COUNTRY, 1992

Socio-economic variables and country	"Don't Know" & "Can't Choose" Responses on Social Structure Questions:				
	Now	30 Years Ago	30 Years from Now	Morally Preferred Structure	Don't Know Index (All)
Education (Yrs)	-.16*	-.14*	-.13*	-.16*	-.18*
Subjective Class	-.05*	-.03*	-.07*	-.05*	-.07*
Gender	.04*	.06*	.06*	.04*	.07*
Age	.06*	-.07*	.08*	.07*	.04*
Out of Labour Force:					
retired	.08*	.07*	.04*	.06*	.08*
unemployed	.02*	.03*	.03*	.02	.03*
housewife	.00	.01	-.02	.01	—
student	.02	.01	.01	.03*	.02
other non-labour force	.03*	.01	.02*	.03*	.03*
Country Dummy Variable (Canada Excluded Category):					
Hungary	-.01	.12*	.13*	.01	.09*
Czech Republic	-.02	.09*	.05*	-.03	.03*
Poland	.06*	.14*	.22*	.08*	.17*
Bulgaria	.09*	.13*	.14*	.08*	.14*
Norway	.00	—	.05*	-.02	.01
New Zealand	-.04*	-.02	-.02	-.03*	-.03*
Philippines	-.07*	-.01	-.01	-.06*	-.04*
R	.32*	.29*	.38*	.31*	.40*
R^2	.10*	.08*	.14*	.10*	.16*
(n)	8710	8710	8710	8710	8710

Significance: F- and t-tests: * $p < .05$.

TABLE 22: REGRESSION OF "DON'T KNOW" INDEX (SOCIAL STRUCTURE
QUESTION) ON SOCIO-ECONOMIC VARIABLES,
BY COUNTRY, 1992

Socio-economic variables	Total	Hungary	Czech Republic	Poland	Bulgaria	Norway	Canada	New Zealand	Philippines
Education (Yrs)	-.19*	-.24*	-.05	-.28*	-.20*	-.11*	-.08*	-.08*	-.02
Subjective Class	.01	-.02	-.04	-.09*	-.11*	-.03	-.07*	-.05	-.08*
Gender	.08*	.10*	.07*	.10*	.04	.08*	.10*	.10*	.00
Age	.04*	.05	-.13*	.04	.03	.04	.10*	.04	.15*
Community Size	@	-.05	-.04	-.05	-.14*	-.03	-.04	-.01	@
Out of Labour Force:									
retired	.11*	.10*	.12*	.03	.09	.12*	.04	-.03	-.01
unemployed	.04*	.04	.03	.01	.07*	.01	.05	.00	.01
housewife	-.03*	.06*	-.01	-.02	.00	.00	.01	-.07*	.01
student	.01	.02	-.01	.04	.05	.00	.04	.01	.00
other non-labour force	.03*	.05	.00	.06*	.06*	.04	.09*	.00	-.04
R	.34*	.39*	.17*	.38*	.41*	.24*	.24*	.15*	.18*
R^2	.12*	.15*	.03*	.15*	.17*	.06*	.06*	.02*	.03*
(n)	8710	1224	1064	1593	1071	1351	906	1154	1182

Significance: F- and t-tests: * $p < .05$;   @ Variable not available.

The general conclusion to both tables is that the "don't know" responses are not randomly distributed within each country sample, but are systematically related to both country and socio-economic background factors, especially those measuring structures of inequality. Respondents who have difficulty coping with the inequality profile questions are more likely to have lower education, to identify with lower social classes, to be women and elderly or retired, and to be out of the labour force. They are more likely to be living in Hungary, the Czech Republic, Poland, and Bulgaria than in Canada, Norway, New Zealand, or the Philippines. It should be emphasized that these inter-country differences are independent of the other socio-economic background variables of education, class, age, gender, and labour force participation. In essence, there is a national cultural differentiation in citizens' ability to answer the inequality profile questions. As much as 16% of the variation in "don't know" responses is explained by such socio-economic and national differences.

The effects of socio-economic factors within countries are explored in Table 22. The most powerful within-country explanation for the "don't knows" appears to be education, especially in Hungary (b =-.24), Poland (b =.28), and Bulgaria (b =-.20). The least educated have the greatest difficulty with these questions. As well, the elderly, women, and rural residents (especially in Bulgaria) show independent effects on "don't know" and "can't choose" responses. It is interesting to note that non-labour force participation seems to have generally stronger effects on "don't know" responses than on the inequality profiles themselves considered earlier in the chapter. The retired in Hungary, the Czech Republic, and Norway, the unemployed in Bulgaria, housewives in Hungary, and "other non-labour force" in Poland, Bulgaria, and Canada seem to evidence high and independent levels of "don't knows."

Two conclusions can be reached from these analyses. First, it is not unreasonable to hypothesize that somewhat stronger explanations of the selection of inequality profiles would have been possible had there had been a greater inclusion of the dispossessed in valid responses to questions. Second, there are strong national cultural differences in respondent difficulties with survey questions in social research, at least in the inequality profiles. These cannot be explained away by class or status differences between nations. This needs to be methodologically and theoretically assessed and studied in future surveys of this nature.

There are marked contrasts in today's world between fact and fantasy, between realities and dreams. As evident from this chapter, in fantasy and dream all citizens are equal. But in fact and reality, there are deep and persisting structures of inequality. One of the enduring passions of social science research has been to observe and explain whether and how the clash between the subjective desire for egalitarianism and the objective structures of inequality are expressed in the potential for social and political action and the formation of groups and organizations devoted to change. Many social scientists have been struck by the irony of social and political inertia in the face of such contradictions. Despite desiring more egalitarian structures, many people are not moved to act; instead, they resign themselves to their present social standing, even though they may want a better society for themselves and their children. There are some hints of an explanation for this inertia in this chapter. Even though positive relations were found between the objective structures and subjective perceptions of inequality, the levels of explained variance are quite low. Since the beginnings of social survey research in the 1940s, social scientists have not found efficient explanations for many social phenomena (like the subjective profiles of inequalities discussed in this chapter). Although there have been modest successes, we have to look for other explanations and more valid measures of the concepts we choose to study. In addition, compared to physical and biological nature, social and political behaviour is in some ways more complex and perhaps more resistant to scientific explanation. This is all the more so in today's global society, as it experiences some of the most profound and accelerated changes in history. We have recently witnessed the breakup of the Communist bloc in Eastern Europe and the former Soviet Union, with profound implications for the economic and political structures, not only of these societies, but of all societies in the world community. In the Western developed counties, citizens are experiencing fundamental changes in job prospects, social attitudes, technological opportunities in communications, and the restructuring of social, economic, and political organizations. Such changes make the adequate explanation of social phenomena more daunting than in stable or stagnant societies. This presents both challenges and barriers for a new generation of social researchers now being trained around the world.

ENDNOTES

1. Thanks are due to Brenda Nussey for assistance in preparing the data for analysis.
2. Percentages total across tables, rather than within tables, for each of the four periods.
3. Each of the five inequality profile questions was scored 1 if the response was affirmative, and 0 if negative. Those selecting "don't know" and "can't choose" were excluded from this part of the analysis. We conduct an analysis of the excluded near the end of the chapter.
4. Years of schooling were coded in all countries (except Canada and Italy) from 0 years to 20 or more years. Canada has unique education categories, which were coded from none (0) through "grade school," "high school," "college," "university," and "graduate school" (8). Italy has a nine-point scale with completely different categories.
5. Codes for job mobility were "much higher than my father" (5), "higher" (4), "about equal" (3), "lower" (2), "much lower than my father" (1).
6. Codes for income mobility were "much better off than my father" (5), "better off" (4), "about equal" (3), "worse off" (2), "much worse off than my father" (1).

7. Codes for education and training mobility were "much better off than my father" (5), "better off" (4), "about equal" (3), "worse off" (2), and "much worse off than my father" (1).
8. Because of the uniqueness of the education measures in Canada and Italy, they could not be brought into the equation in conjunction with the country dummy variables.
9. Community size categories were unique to each country. They were coded into four to eight categories, depending on country. The highest score was assigned to the largest urban region; the lowest to the rural areas. Strictly speaking, they are not comparable across countries. No such variable was available for the Philippines. For all the countries taken together, a simple urban/rural dichotomy common to all countries was used.
10. Trade union membership could not be analysed for Italy, New Zealand, and the Philippines.
11. See, for example, P. Gurin, who notes that "American polls taken since the early 1960s have always shown that men are somewhat more supportive than women of role equality" (1985, 152).
12. The remaining responses were divided between those who neither agreed nor disagreed and those who could not choose.

REFERENCES

Evans, Geoffrey. (1993). Is Gender on the 'New Agenda'? A Comparative Analysis of the Politicization of Inequality Between Men and Women. *European Journal of Political Research, 24,* 135-58.

Evans, M.D.R., Jonathan Kelly, & Tamas Kolosi. (1992). Images of Class: Public Perceptions in Hungary and Australia. *American Sociological Review, 57,* 461-82.

Gurin, P. (1985). Women's Gender Consciousness. *Public Opinion Quarterly, 49,* 143-63.

Hayes, Bernadette C. (1995). The Impact of Class on Political Attitudes: A Comparative Study of Great Britain, West Germany, Australia, and the United States. *European Journal of Political Research, 27,* 69-91.

Kelly, Jonathan, & M.D.R. Evans. (1995). Class and Class Conflict in Six Western Nations. *American Sociological Review, 60,* 157-78.

CHAPTER FOUR

GETTING AHEAD AROUND THE WORLD

Jon H. Pammett

BELIEFS ABOUT SOCIAL MOBILITY are a crucial psychological dimension of social inequality in any country. Liberal ideology accepts that inequality of condition may exist, but that equality of opportunity will allow individuals to advance to the limits of their ability. If the channels for such personal advancement are open and widely used, a situation of social inequity of condition may be widely accepted in any society. In fact, such a situation may be actually desired, since material gains will be the product of personal achievement and thus considered deserved. The opportunities for benefits provide, according to liberalism, the dynamic for society as a whole to prosper, since all individuals operate in their own rational self-interest in the attempt to accumulate more goods. However, if the inequalities in society are not seen as natural ones, but rather imposed by the powerful and the privileged, their acceptance is much more problematic (Grabb, 1984, 8; Goldthorpe, 1987, chapter 1).

With the collapse of communism at the beginning of the current decade, this liberal belief system has arguably spread around the world. Societies where those advocating collectivist ideologies were in power have undergone the processes of marketization and privatization. But it is unclear whether the official emphasis on individual achievement and free enterprise that has gone along with this restructuring has met with either acceptance or approval in formerly communist states. In addition, states where social democratic beliefs are widespread may not have a belief structure that emphasizes the rewards that await gifted or hardworking individuals. Great Britain, for example, had social democratic governments during earlier decades (the 1960s and 1970s), but has undergone a sustained period of conservative governance. The British political elite may have taken the country in a rightward direction, but what of the attitudes of the population? Are liberal (sometimes called "neoconservative") values accepted by the population as the constraints within which they have to work to secure a living? The ISSP survey can give us a number of approaches to this important subject.

Regardless of the political organization of modern states, we will be interested in knowing which factors are considered to be most important for "getting ahead in life." The question that we will be examining asks respondents to comment on several suggested items that affect "opportunities for getting ahead." Such a question structure, of course, does not directly measure the respondents' attitudes toward these things, but rather how important they assess them to be in reality. So, after seeing what factors are rated as important in success, we will employ a number of measures of people's own beliefs about the desirable organization of society.

INDIVIDUAL DRIVE AND ABILITY

Four factors in this category are measured by the battery of items asked in the ISSP surveys in 1992 in 18 countries. *Natural ability* taps the innate characteristics possessed by a person, while *ambition* adds a value or motivational dimension. Someone who gets ahead by virtue of either natural ability or ambition may also be engaging in *hard work*, another factor measured here. However, hardworking people can sometimes succeed simply by dint of this activity, overcoming obstacles posted by rather modest gifts of ability. Finally, people can be more likely to get ahead in life if they have a *good education*. Educational opportunities are of course not perfectly related to ability, and can be more available to those from higher social classes. Nevertheless, successfully taking advantage of an educational opportunity is itself a mark of individual achievement.

FAMILY BACKGROUND

People can get ahead in life for the "accidental" reason of having come from an advantaged background. Thus *coming from a wealthy family* provides a head start in terms of resources, and *having well-educated parents* provides a greater likelihood of wealth, but also motivation to achieve educational goals, which is in turn related to success.

CONNECTIONS

Knowing the right people can undoubtedly be an important step on the ladder of success for any person, even those who have ability on their own. In a different vein, *having political connections* may provide opportunities for advancement by way of patronage. Societies in which these factors are ranked near the top in importance for advancement are downplaying the liberal ideals of the first category mentioned above, relating to personal achievement. Similarly, in some countries the nature or direction of a *person's political beliefs* may be important in how much advancement is possible, or which doors are opened.

SOCIODEMOGRAPHICS

Finally, societies may show a perception that a number of ascriptive characteristics are major determinants of the ability to succeed. *A person's race* or *a person's religion* may be influential, as may *the region* a person grew up in, or whether someone was born *a man or woman.* In many societies, factors such as these impose limits on the distance a person is able to go in life, or at least may provide obstacles to success.

The fourfold classification of the important elements of success is based on confirmatory factor analyses undertaken on the survey data from all eighteen countries available in the ISSP. While there is some occasional variation in the number of factors produced by the thirteen items from country to country, there is substantial commonality in the structure of the factor analysis. For example, "knowing the right people" usually produces a factor together with "political connections," rather than with "coming from a wealthy family," and thus we consider it a measure of *connections* rather than *background.*

An initial investigation of the public's views about the important elements influencing advancement in several countries begins with Table 1. Four Western countries are presented: Canada, Great Britain, the United States, and West Germany. For the last three of these, data is also available from the ISSP survey carried out in 1987. It should be noted that the 1992 German sample was only chosen from the former West of that country, even though reunification had already taken place.

It is clear that in all these countries, *individual* factors predominate in public opinion about what is important to get ahead in life. There is some variation, however, among the particular factors within the individualistic

TABLE 1: MOST IMPORTANT FACTORS FOR GETTING AHEAD,
CANADA, GREAT BRITAIN, UNITED STATES, AND WEST GERMANY,
1992 AND 1987. (MEAN RANKINGS)

	Canada	Great Britain		United States		West Germany	
	1992*	1992	1987	1992	1987	1992	1987
INDIVIDUAL							
ambition	1	2	3	1	2	2	2
natural ability	4	4	4	4	4	3	5
hard work	3	1	1	2	1	4	4
good education	2	3	2	3	3	1	1
CONNECTIONS							
knowing right people	5	5	5	5	5	5	3
political connections	8	11	11	7	8	8	9
political beliefs	11	10	13	11	12	9	11
BACKGROUND							
well-educated parents	6	6	6	6	6	6	6
wealthy family	7	7	7	8	7	7	7
SOCIODEMOGRAPHICS							
gender	9	9	9	9	10	11	10
race	9	8	8	10	9	10	8
religion	12	13	12	12	11	12	12
region	10	12	10	12	13	13	13

* 1992 is only year available for Canada.

category. In Canada and the United States, "ambition" leads the way, whereas this factor, which perhaps most clearly exemplifies the free-enterprise spirit, is only in second place in Great Britain and Germany. The British are more convinced that "hard work" is the key to success, while the Germans believe that "having a good education" is most important. These differences, however, are those of degree, since Canadians, British, and Americans all rate education among the top three factors for success, and similarly, Canadians, Americans, and Germans are almost as convinced of the value of hard work as are the British.

Close behind the individual factors in providing the key to success is one of our measures of *connections*, namely the value of "knowing the right people." This factor was ranked fifth in 1992 among the four countries we are examining at the moment, and was in fact the third most important factor in West Germany in the previous survey in 1987. Table 1 shows that the public prefers to think of connections in terms of simply "knowing" others who might help them rather than overtly in terms of "political connections," a factor ranked a few notches below. "Political connections," a much more direct indicator of favouritism, is ranked seventh in the United States, and eighth in Canada and Germany, indicating a widespread belief that natural ability is not the only determinant of advancement, and that politics takes a role. "A person's political beliefs" are ranked toward the bottom of the list in all countries. However, it is worth knowing that in Great Britain, the United States, and Germany, "political beliefs" were thought to be more important in 1992 than they were five years previously.

The third category of factors, those measuring *family background*, is placed just behind "knowing the right people" in the belief structure of all four of the countries in Table 1. "Having well-educated parents" and "coming from a wealthy family" measure two different aspects of the social class and/or status structure in a society. Wealth represents the direct material stake in life that a person will inherit (literally as well as figuratively). It can of course provide the connections we have noted above. It ensures access to various important institutions of society, including the educational ones, given a modicum of natural ability. Parental education is somewhat broader in scope, in that it provides knowledge and ensures a more intellectual home environment, which in turn stimulates the capacities of individuals. Well-educated parents are more likely to provide educational opportunities for their children, which in turn makes it more likely that they will achieve material and other successes in life.

Factors in the *sociodemographic* category are generally ranked at the bottom of the list of potential influences on life achievement. In Canada, Great Britain, and the United States "being born a man or a woman" is recognized as having an effect, but the mean scores reveal that this item is typically rated by respondents as being "not very important" in determining whether or not one gets ahead in life. (Women, however, are somewhat more convinced of its importance, as chapter 7 of this volume points out.) In the United States, contrary to what we might expect, "a person's race" is not thought to be the most important of the sociodemographic factors; more respondents think race is "not very important" than feel it plays an significant part in success. The same can be said for "the region of the country a person grew up in," which is often thought to be related to achievement in Canada, especially among those who think that certain provinces are favoured when government jobs are being distributed. Finally, in none of our sample countries does "a person's religion" appear to play a significant part in achieving success, at least according to public opinion.

An initial conclusion, therefore, is that when it comes to a recipe for advancement in life, people believe that those who make it do so on the basis of their own ability, their educational training, and their capacity for hard work. Giving a boost to this personal initiative and achievement would be the luck involved in being born into a wealthy or well-educated family, and the opportunity to develop personal contacts with the "right people." Despite much publicity to the contrary, people in general do not believe that sociodemographic factors such as gender, race, religion, or region of origin play much of a role in inhibiting the achievement of their goals.

How far has the dominance of personal initiative as the prime producer of success spread around the world? We can get a good indicator of this from Table 2, which displays the six top-ranked factors for getting ahead in all eighteen countries available in the ISSP studies for 1992. In every case, the main factors appear to be those in the category of *individual drive and initiative*. For most Western European and North American countries, the top four factors in getting ahead are all from this category. There is, to be sure, some variation in the way in which the four are ranked. In Canada, the United States, Norway, and Sweden, "ambition" is the primary key to success. As we have already noted, the British rank "hard work" first, although Table 2 shows that they are alone among Western countries in doing so. For some others, like Germany, Austria, and Italy, "a good education" is considered more important.

In some countries, *connections* are seen as especially meaningful when it comes to getting ahead in life. Among Western countries, Italy ranks such factors highest, with "knowing the right people" in third position, and "political connections" sixth. However, the 1987 results for Italy actually placed these two factors a notch higher; at that time, "knowing the right people" was second in overall importance, right after "having a good education" (Smith, 1989, 68). This finding provides evidence that Italian political culture emphasizes connections more than, for example, "hard work," which is ranked fifth. Interestingly, however, the one country in Table 2 that rates "knowing the right people" higher than Italy is Russia. This is probably less an innate characteristic of Russians than a residue of the control of political institutions by the Communist Party. In 1992, Russians were convinced that, along with their natural ability and their capacity for hard work, they still needed to know somebody in order to get ahead in life. Most of the former communist states in the ISSP rank connections somewhat higher than do Western countries. Thus, East

TABLE 2: MOST IMPORTANT FACTORS FOR GETTING AHEAD IN LIFE IN EIGHTEEN COUNTRIES

	1	2	3	4	5	6
Canada	ambition	good eduction	hard work	natural ability	knowing people	well-ed parents
USA	ambition	hard work	good education	natural ability	knowing people	well-ed parents
Britain	hard work	ambition	good education	natural ability	knowing people	well-ed parents
W. Germany	good education	ambition	natural ability	hard work	knowing people	well-ed parents
Austria	good eduction	ambition	natural ability	hard work	knowing people	pol connections
Italy	good education	natural ability	knowing people	ambition	hard work	pol connections
Netherlands	ambition	hard work	good education	natural ability	knowing people	race
Sweden	ambition	hard * work	good * education	natural ability	knowing people	well-ed parents
New Zealand	ambition	good eduction	natural ability	well-ed parents	knowing people	wealthy family
E. Germany	good education	ambition	hard work	knowing people	natural ability	well-ed parents
Hungary	ambition	natural ability	hard work	knowing people	good education	wealthy family
Czech Rep.	hard work	ambition	natural ability	knowing people	good education	wealthy family
Slovakia	ambition	good education	natural ability	knowing people	hard work	well-ed parents
Poland	natural ability	hard work	ambition	knowing people	good education	wealthy family
Bulgaria	ambition	hard work	good * education	natural* ability	knowing people	wealthy family
Russia	natural ability	knowing people	hard work	good education	ambition	wealthy family
Philippines	hard work	good education	ambition	natural ability	well-ed parents	knowing people

* Equal scores

Germany, Hungary, the Czech Republic, Slovenia, and Poland put "knowing the right people" in fourth position, rather than the fifth place ranking most common in the West.

IS INEQUALITY JUSTIFIED?

The individualistic liberal believes that he or she can get ahead by virtue of personal effort or qualities. We have seen that respondents in all the countries of the ISSP survey feel that the reward structure emphasizes these factors. It is not clear from the data contained in Tables 1 and 2, however, whether respondents are convinced that the reward structure of society *should* be organized to maximize the fruits of these individual labours. One could imagine a belief system in which a person considers it important that substantial financial gain should accompany individual achievement, even if this means that others in society suffer hardship. This would involve an acceptance of a social structure of inequality, in that much greater rewards would go to those who, by dint of their personal efforts, were able to succeed, as opposed to those granted to the "failures." If such beliefs were widespread, they would provide a powerful explanation for the continued existence of social inequality—the people want it.

Several items are available in the ISSP studies that allow us to investigate this possibility. Initially, we can see that the citizens of all countries surveyed are generally of the opinion that "money counts." The ISSP samples were asked how strongly they agreed or disagreed with the idea that people would only be willing to put in extra effort of various sorts if they were paid extra for doing so. Table 3 shows the results with regard to three such things: taking extra responsibility; getting skills and qualifications; and studying for years to become a lawyer or doctor. The questions used in Table 3 and the two subsequent tables are in a five-point agree-disagree format, ranging from "strongly agree" (coded 1) to "strongly disagree" (coded 5). Thus, the general mean scores for countries displayed in these tables indicate agreement if less than the neutral point of 3, and disagreement if over 3.

All the countries surveyed had majorities of respondents who felt that financial incentives were necessary for their fellow citizens to take on extra responsibilities, develop skills, and pursue studies. However, there is considerable variation observable in Table 3 about how much such extra pay mattered. In particular, many of the post-communist countries, like Bulgaria, Russia, Poland, and Hungary, contain populations that are quite

TABLE 3: IMPORTANCE OF FINANCIAL INCENTIVES
IN EIGHTEEN COUNTRIES, 1992
(MEAN AGREE/DISAGREE, 1-5)

Importance of being paid extra to:

	take extra responsibility	get skills & qualifications	study to be lawyer/doctor
Canada	2.51	2.85	2.47
United States	2.44	2.71	2.27
Great Britain	2.17	2.43	2.25
West Germany	2.29	2.17	1.78
Austria	2.30	2.10	1.76
Italy	1.87	2.03	2.11
Norway	2.49	2.85	2.40
Sweden	2.17	2.30	2.18
Australia	2.17	2.26	1.98
New Zealand	2.27	2.56	2.22
East Germany	2.33	2.28	1.88
Hungary	2.45	2.52	2.43
Czech Republic	2.40	2.51	2.46
Slovenia	2.21	2.38	2.27
Poland	1.96	2.13	2.02
Bulgaria	1.48	1.55	1.61
Russia	1.53	2.09	2.36
Philippines	2.58	2.59	2.42

convinced that people will not take on these extra burdens without being financially compensated. It is not clear, however, whether such convictions stem from a general embracing of individualistic liberal values, or from experience with the previous communist system. One of the charges most frequently made about communism was that it limited productivity by not rewarding individual work sufficiently. It may be that in reaction to a stifling work atmosphere that prevailed for the lifetimes of most respondents, people are here asserting their belief that more individual rewards are important to improve the work ethic.

The Western European and North American countries for which we have evidence also view the importance of financial incentives somewhat differently. Italians, for example, are more likely to strongly agree that extra pay is important to get people to take extra responsibility at work than are citizens of other Western countries. However, when it comes to "study[ing] for years to become a doctor or a lawyer" Germans and Austrians are more likely to believe that no one would want to do that "unless they expected to earn a lot more than ordinary workers." In Norway, on the other hand, extra money is not thought to be as necessary to induce people to upgrade their skills and take more responsibility as it is elsewhere. It is interesting to note in this regard that North Americans appear to be less concerned with such financial incentives than are Europeans. Overall, considering the three mean scores in Table 3, Canadians appear to be least dependent on extra pay to apply themselves to their work and education. They are closely followed by Americans and Filipinos in their willingness to do more regardless of monetary incentives. It must be remembered, however, that the mean scores for these countries are still on the "agree" side of the neutral point. Perhaps the connection between financial inducements and extra work and study undertakings are still there in these countries, but are less overtly connected with "extra pay" than they are in the former communist societies and in Western Europe.

It is some distance, however, from thinking that financial incentives are necessary for individuals to take more of an interest in increasing their own workload to approving a society in which there are major degrees of inequality. In Table 4 we see that, when asked whether "large differences in income are necessary for [national] prosperity," public attitudes in almost all countries surveyed tended toward disagreement. Taking account of the possibility that the use of the word "large" in the question to characterize the extent of the income differences may have triggered the negative responses here, it is still important to note that there is, in general, a lack of enthusiasm for an overtly unequal society, one in which there are wide disparities in wealth. It appears that people in most countries are willing to approve a certain amount of inequality in wealth and income, but balk when the differences reach major dimensions. Additional evidence that there are suspicions about the utility of wide income differentials can be found in the second column of Table 4. Here, the respondents were asked about the extent of their agreement or disagreement with the suggestion that "allowing business to make good profits is the best way to improve everyone's standard of living." While the mean score on this item is slightly on the "agree" side in most countries (though not in Russia and Eastern Germany), it hovers around the neutral mark (a mean of 3). There is therefore for many people no direct connection between business profit and national prosperity. Cautious acceptance of the operation of the commercial sector is the best way to describe this public attitude. And when inequalities threaten to get out of hand, public opinion turns negative.

TABLE 4: AGREEMENT WITH PROSPERITY/BUSINESS EXPLANATIONS
FOR INEQUALITY IN EIGHTEEN COUNTRIES, 1992
(MEAN AGREEMENT, 1-5)

	Large differences in income are necessary for national prosperity.	Allowing business to make good profits is the best way to improve everyone's standard of living.
Canada	3.67	2.99
United States	3.33	2.83
Great Britain	3.49	2.88
West Germany	3.48	2.99
Austria	3.68	2.90
Italy	3.25	2.53
Norway	3.60	2.90
Sweden	3.12	2.77
Australia	3.24	2.67
New Zealand	3.60	2.84
Eeat Germany	3.83	3.10
Hungary	3.59	2.76
Czech Republic	3.30	2.69
Slovenia	3.26	2.54
Poland	3.12	2.27
Bulgaria	3.60	2.62
Russia	3.39	3.06
Philippines	2.49	2.77

A CLASS BASIS FOR INEQUALITY?

We have seen that there is little support for tracing the origins of social inequality to a widespread public demand for major differences in wealth to provide an engine for national prosperity and growth. Alternative explanations are based on the ability of privileged groups to construct a social and economic system to maximize their own advantage, and the inability of ordinary people to do anything about it. In general, there is considerable agreement that such "class based" explanations for the existence of inequality have merit. The mean scores on agreement with the statement that "inequality continues because it benefits the rich and powerful" are close to the 2 mark ("agree") in most countries. Citizens of Western countries are almost as willing to accept this explanation as are those of the former communist states. For example, only 23% of Americans, 19% of Canadians, and 18% of British respondents disagree with it in any way. Even the slightly more Marxist-sounding statement that "inequality continues because ordinary people don't join together to

TABLE 5: AGREEMENT WITH CLASS EXPLANATIONS FOR
INEQUALITY IN EIGHTEEN COUNTRIES,
1992 (MEAN AGREEMENT, 1-5)

Inequality continues because ...

	it benefits the rich and powerful	ordinary people don't join together to get rid of it
Canada	2.33	2.81
United States	2.51	2.75
Great Britain	2.32	2.91
West Germany	2.12	2.80
Austria	2.27	2.68
Italy	2.08	2.39
Norway	2.23	2.83
Sweden	2.53	2.98
Australia	2.43	3.05
New Zealand	2.40	3.00
East Germany	1.83	2.68
Hungary	2.66	3.16
Czech Republic	2.49	2.73
Slovenia	2.24	2.75
Poland	2.13	2.58
Bulgaria	1.78	2.49
Russia	1.97	2.90
Philippines	2.69	2.66

get rid of it" has a surprising degree of agreement in Western countries. For example, in the United States and Canada only about 30% of respondents to the ISSP study disagreed with that statement at all, and very few of these disagreed strongly.

Full acceptance of a class-based explanation for inequality necessitates a recognition that conflict is a natural state of affairs, particularly conflict between groups defined according to their economic status, position, or viability in any society. Table 6 shows that the citizens of all countries surveyed are prone to recognize the existence of various kinds of conflict between groups in their societies, but that attitudes vary considerably when it comes to defining the seriousness of these conflicts. The mean scores displayed in Table 6 are out of four, rather than five, as in previous tables. Thus, the mean scores for Canada of 2.47 in reference to the strength of conflict between the poor and the rich, 2.71 regarding the unemployed and those with jobs, and 2.28 between management and workers all indicate opinion between "strong conflict" (2) and "not very strong conflict" (3). In two countries, Hungary and the United States,

TABLE 6: OPINIONS ABOUT THE STRENGTH OF CONFLICT IN EIGHTEEN
COUNTRIES, 1992 (MEAN /4)

Conflict between ...	Poor/ Rich	Unemployed/ Employed	Management/ Workers
Canada	2.47	2.71	2.28
United States	2.13	2.43	2.23
Great Britain	2.28	2.51	2.44
West Germany	2.63	2.66	2.47
Austria	2.81	2.67	2.71
Italy	2.33	2.44	2.49
Norway	2.92	2.91	2.79
Sweden	2.71	3.03	2.79
Australia	2.65	2.68	2.52
New Zealand	2.38	2.49	2.43
Eeat Germany	2.23	2.50	2.13
Hungary	2.07	2.53	2.21
Czech Republic	2.78	3.01	2.47
Slovenia	2.63	2.79	2.10
Poland	2.38	2.78	2.55
Bulgaria	2.44	2.85	2.50
Russia	2.25	3.18	2.51
Philippines	2.37	2.62	2.43

mean scores close to 2 (2.07 and 2.13 respectively) show that there is
more recognition of friction between the rich and the poor. Americans,
Canadians, and citizens of three Eastern European countries (the former
East Germany, Hungary, and Slovenia) are also prone to thinking that
conflicts between management and workers are deep ones.

THE ROLE OF GOVERNMENT

We have seen that respondents in all countries for which we have data recognize the existence of social inequalities and conflicts, though they may
differ in diagnosing their causes and in assessing their seriousness. What,
if anything, should be done about them? In particular, what is the role of
the state in alleviating the disparities between those with high and low
incomes, and in locating or providing employment for those without
jobs? This is an instance where we might expect differences in philoso-
phy between citizens of post-communist states and those from Western
Europe and North America. Under the communist regimes, the government directed the economic activity of these states, and in most cases
attempted to ensure full employment for workers to provide a set level of
income. In the West, there have also been certain differences in the policy

approaches of governments in various states according to whether social democratic parties or conservative parties were in power. New Zealand, Great Britain, and West Germany are three cases in point here. Though in all three cases conservative parties were in power at the time of the 1992 ISSP surveys, public opinion in all of these countries was substantially favourable to social democratic political ideas.

Table 7 displays three measures of public opinion about various roles for government. Respondents indicated on a five-point scale their agreement or disagreement with the statements that government should 1) "reduce the differences in income between people with high incomes and those with low incomes"; 2) "provide a job for everyone who wants one"; and 3) "provide everyone with a guaranteed basic income." These three policy positions have been associated with the ideology of communist states, particularly with regard to providing jobs and assuring a basic income. Social democratic parties in Western countries have been most associated with the first proposition, to reduce income differentials, and also to some extent with guaranteeing a basic income. While Western governments have often made job creation a priority, they have usually shied away in recent years from commitments to provide jobs for all through direct government action.

We can observe from Table 7 that there are indeed substantial differences between countries with respect to the desire for governments to take action to reduce social inequalities and provide jobs and a basic income. It is notable that the North American countries, the United States and Canada, are the most negative on government intervention to reduce inequality. On two of the three items, Americans have mean scores over 3, indicating an overall disagreement with the propositions. Canadians are actually more negative than Americans to the suggestion that government should provide jobs for everyone, though the mean score for both countries is marginally on the positive side of neutral.

The enthusiasm for government endeavour to reduce social inequalities comes mainly from the post-communist countries, particularly Russia, Bulgaria, Hungary, and Poland. In these states, the population expresses itself strongly in favour when the suggestion is made that government needs to provide jobs for all, and ensure that everyone has a basic annual income. There is, however, less agreement in the post-communist countries that it is the responsibility of government to reduce differentials between those with high and low incomes. Although the mean scores for the four countries listed above indicate that the population in general

TABLE 7: OPINIONS ABOUT GOVERNMENT IN EIGHTEEN
COUNTRIES, 1992
(MEAN AGREEMENT/DISAGREEMENT 1/5)

Government should ...	Reduce income differences	Provide jobs for all	Provide basic income
Canada	2.77	2.96	2.83
United States	3.07	2.86	3.25
Great Britain	2.33	2.53	2.34
West Germany	2.40	2.36	2.60
Austria	2.24	2.15	2.79
Italy	1.92	1.64	2.24
Norway	2.53	1.95	2.01
Sweden	2.69	2.13	2.89
Australia	2.93	2.97	2.75
New Zealand	2.69	2.70	2.51
East Germany	1.74	1.56	1.71
Hungary	2.07	1.71	1.70
Czech Republic	2.36	2.03	2.31
Slovenia	2.01	1.94	2.09
Poland	2.08	1.67	1.74
Bulgaria	1.76	1.57	1.42
Russia	2.35	1.38	1.45
Philippines	2.51	1.88	1.90

agrees with this role for government, approval is more restrained. It is interesting to note that the population of the Eastern part of Germany, separated in the ISSP survey in 1992, is very similar in its attitudes to government activity to the populations of the other post-communist states on these items. East Germans look quite dissimilar to West Germans when defining the appropriate degree of government intervention in their lives.

Western European countries generally show levels of agreement with government action to reduce social inequalities that are more favourable than North Americans but less so than the Eastern countries. There are, however, some exceptions to this generalization. Italy, for example, is quite positive toward government action for this purpose, more so than the other Western European countries, and also more favourable than the Czech Republic and Slovenia. Sweden, long a bastion of social democratic policies to reduce income differentials and provide basic services, has a population less supportive of these actions than the British, for example.

TABLE 8: PREDICTORS OF OPINION FAVOURING GOVERNMENT
ACTION TO REDUCE INCOME DIFFERENTIALS,
EIGHTEEN COUNTRIES, 1992

(multiple regression)	Canada	United States	Great Britain	West Germany	Austria	Italy
Getting Ahead						
Ambition	-.07	-.12*	-.08*	-.01	-.01	-.07
Hard Work	-.12*	-.05	.01	-.08*	-.04	-.01
Natural Ability	.05	.01	-.02	.03	.08	.01
Good Education	.01	-.07	.03	-.07*	-.05	.01
Knowing People	.04	.06	.14*	.02	.07	.09*
Well-educated Parents	.02	.04	-.07	.03	.03	.04
Incentives						
No Study Unless						
More Pay	.06	.08*	.06	.03	.03	.05
Ideology						
Large Income						
Differentials Necessary	-.12*	-.03	-.16*	-.10*	-.06	-.07
Ordinary People						
Don't Get Rid						
of Inequality	.20*	.21*	.21*	.19*	.18*	.11*
Strong Conflict						
Poor/Rich	.26*	.23*	.23*	.15*	.07	.17*
Taxes on High						
Incomes too High	-.15*	-.04	-.16*	-.22*	-.23*	-.25*
Multiple R	.46	.41	.51	.43	.37	.39
Adjusted R square	.20	.16	.25	.18	.13	.14

	Norway	Sweden	Australia	New Zealand	East Germany	Hungary
Getting Ahead						
Ambition	.01	-.02	-.07*	-.06	.04	.01
Hard Work	.01	.05	-.01	-.07	-.03	.03
Natural Ability	-.01	-.00	.00	.03	.00	.10*
Good Education	-.01	-.00	-.03	-.03	.06	-.04
Knowing People	.07*	.05	.04	.06	-.00	.09*
Well-ed Parents	-.06	.01	.11*	.02	.01	.02
Incentives						
No Study Unless						
More Pay	.12*	.16*	.06*	.08*	.07	.11*

(multiple regression)	Norway	Sweden	Aus-tralia	New Zealand	East Germany	Hungary
Ideology						
Large Income Differentials Necessary	-.30*	-.31*	-.26*	-.08*	-.11*	-.18*
Ordinary People Don't Get Rid of Inequality	.16*	.21*	.22*	.19*	.14*	.19*
Strong Conflict Poor/Rich	.14*	.10*	.13*	.21*	.16*	.15*
Taxes on High Incomes too High	-.24*	-.21*	-.21*	-.25*	-.15*	-.11*
Multiple R	.59	.60	.52	.48	.37	.41
Adjusted R square	.34	.34	.26	.23	.12	.16

	Czech	Slovenia	Poland	Bulgaria	Russia	Philippines
Getting Ahead						
Ambition	.05	-.12*	-.04	-.02	.04	-.07
Hard Work	-.05	-.04	.04	.00	-.03	.04
Natural Ability	-.06	.06	.02	-.01	.07	.02
Good Education	-.04	.00	-.03	-.03	-.03	.05
Knowing People	-.04	.08	.02	.01	-.03	.03
Well-educated Parents	.03	.03	.07	.06	.00	-.03
Incentives						
No Study Unless More Pay	.04	.13*	.01	.06	.05	.08*
Ideology						
Large Income Differentials Necessary	-.20*	-.18*	-.16*	-.24*	-.11*	-.06
Ordinary People Don't Get Rid of Inequality	.33*	.21*	.31*	.37*	.31*	.14*
Strong Conflict Poor/Rich	.13*	.18*	.14*	.10*	.04	.04
Taxes on High Incomes too High	-.10*	-.10*	-.17*	-.07	-.10*	.05
Multiple R	.47	.45	.46	.49	.39	.21
Adjusted R square	.21	.18	.20	.23	.14	.04

*significant @.01

Many of the attitudes we have been examining in this chapter can be used as predictors of respondents' opinions about the proper role of government in reducing income differentials. Table 8 displays the results of multiple regression analyses in which the dependent variable is agreement or disagreement with the proposition that "it is the responsibility of government to reduce the differences in income between people with high incomes and those with low incomes." We have already seen in Table 7 that the citizenry of countries in the survey differ in their opinions on this, ranging from some post-communist states, which are quite favourable, to North American states, which are more sceptical. Regardless of country, however, many of the same factors are significantly related to individual opinions about the proper role of government in income redistribution.

A number of the factors ranked as important in *getting ahead in life* (Tables 1 and 2) might be expected to be significantly related to favouring the reduction of income differences. Those people who think that individual qualities, like ambition, or individual actions, like hard work, are important in getting ahead in their countries are hypothesized to be unfavourable to government action to reduce the ability of such hardworking people to earn more money without it being redistributed to others. Indeed, we find in Table 8 that in Western countries like Canada, the United States, Great Britain, and West Germany, this hypothesis is supported. In the countries just mentioned, either "ambition" or "hard work" has a significant negative relation to support for government action. In the post-communist states, only Hungary and Slovenia show a significant relationship between a belief in the importance of individual actions and a distrust of government action.

The other one of the *getting ahead* variables that has a significant relation to opinion on government action in some countries is "knowing the right people." Here, the signs are positive rather than negative, indicating that people who thought that connections were important in getting ahead are more likely to believe that the state should be acting to reduce income differentials. Great Britain, Italy, Norway, and Hungary are the four countries where this relationship reaches statistical significance. In these countries it is reasonable to assume that people who think that knowing the right people helps someone get ahead in life are displeased that such is the case, and feel that government should be moving to counteract this tendency.

A variable measuring the importance of *incentives* (Table 3) is also important in some nations when it comes to predicting public attitudes on income redistribution. The measure used is the question that asked people whether they agreed or disagreed with the proposition that "no-one would study for years to become a lawyer or doctor unless they expected to earn a lot more than ordinary workers." Once again, the signs of the relationship between this attitude and the dependent variable in Table 8 are positive, indicating that people who agree that doctors and lawyers expected to earn a lot more felt that government should undertake more income redistribution, presumably to take some of those extra earnings away from such highly paid professionals. Countries as diverse as Sweden, the United States, Hungary, and the Philippines illustrate the presence of this relationship.

The strongest predictors of public support for state action in virtually every country in the ISSP study are attitudes measuring aspects of ideology, not surprising given the fact that the dependent variable has ideological overtones itself. People who believe that "large income differences are necessary for national prosperity" (Table 4) are not as favourable to state action to reduce them, and those who feel that "taxes on high incomes are too high" share this belief that government should not be redistributing the income they see remaining after the tax bite. Other attitudinal predictors that are significant in most countries are the belief that there is "strong conflict between the rich and the poor," and that "inequality persists because ordinary people don't join together to get rid of it." This group of ideological measures does the lion's share of the work in the regression equations displayed in Table 8, resulting in moderate totals of explained variance.

There exists in most countries we are examining a reasonably coherent structure of attitudes toward the role of government in alleviating social inequality. Those people who are strongly committed to the idea that personal initiative is the key to success are less supportive of government action. Those who feel that the well-off are being taxed unfairly or that the opportunity for some to make much more money than others is necessary to the health of the economy have a similar antipathy to an activist role for the state. On the other hand, people who think that factors like family background or connections allow some lucky ones to succeed while others fail believe that it is the responsibility of governments to redistribute wealth to some extent. If people think that the society is full of conflict between the poor and the rich, and that ordinary people should get together to create a more egalitarian society, they also believe that the state should act to reduce social inequality.

◆

The data from the ISSP survey analyzed in this chapter have demonstrated that people in many countries recognize that their ability to succeed in life is primarily dependent on their own initiative and abilities. This necessitates the existence of social inequalities, especially since wage differentials are important in motivating work activity, a point of view particularly apparent in the post-communist countries. However, other factors combine with individual ambition, hard work, and qualifications to allow people to get ahead. Family background, connections, and also some considerations like gender can affect success rates.

People in general are willing to reward success, but do not want a society in which the inequalities are wide chasms, particularly when it comes to the distribution of wealth. Where such major inequalities do exist, public opinion believes that this is because the rich and powerful have managed to structure things to their benefit. Rather than being a desirable state of affairs, necessitated by the overall benefits derived by society, they feel that inequalities in society are perpetuated because the ordinary people do not rise up to get rid of them.

Faced with inequalities, people differ on what to do. In the post-communist countries, many feel that government should act to reduce income differentials, and also to provide jobs and a basic annual income. In North America, however, government is not given such a public mandate. In all countries, the people who support state action to reduce inequalities are those who feel that equality of opportunity is interfered with by inherited wealth, family background, or political connections, or who see the rich exploiting the poor by taking income far beyond their entitlements. Elements of liberalism as a belief system are pervasive throughout the world, but the populations of all countries are uncomfortable when disparities in wealth become too great, when the poor are exploited, or when equality of opportunity is threatened.

REFERENCES

Goldthorpe, John H. (1987). *Social Mobility and Class Structure in Modern Britain.* Oxford: Clarendon Press.

Grabb, Edward G. (1984). *Social Inequality: Classical and Contemporary Theorists.* Toronto: Holt, Rinehart and Winston.

Smith, Tom. (1989). Inequality and Welfare. In Roger Jowell, Sharon Witherspoon, & Lindsay Brook (Eds.), *British Social Attitudes: Special International Report* (59-86). Aldershot: Gower.

CHAPTER FIVE

CANADIAN PUBLIC PERCEPTIONS OF INEQUALITY DIRECTIONS AND POLICY IMPLICATIONS

Scott Bennett

TODAY, THE CANADIAN PUBLIC is faced with public policy discourse that is framed in terms of the demands associated with various segments of the population. These segments *might* be defined in cultural, ethnic, or linguistic terms. Examples of these types of groups are French speakers, English speakers, ethnic minorities, and aboriginals. Alternatively, they *might* be defined by their demographic or socio-economic characteristics, such as gender, income, occupation, or family type. It is also true that some perceptions of policy entitlement focus on regional or provincial segments of the country. However, some parts of the Canadian community are more explicitly represented by organized interest groups than others, and these clearly dominate current public policy considerations. This paper examines the way the public sees the inequality experienced by various segments of the Canadian political community, and the reasons for such perceptions. The way the public perceives inequality is an important element in the process of establishing the legitimacy of claims to entitlement when public policy initiatives are constructed.[1]

In public policy design, a distinction is made between universal policy and targeted policy. In fact, these concepts define the extremes of a varied spectrum of options. At one extreme, we find programs that maintain a common standard or make up deficiencies with respect to such a standard, and require that these standards apply to all. Perhaps hospital and medical care and early forms of some income transfers once approached this extreme. At the end of the spectrum associated with extreme targeting, we find very particularistic policies defined by contractual arrangements between the state and a person or corporate entity. For example, there are specific arrangements with individuals, private firms, or NGOs to build roads, construct buildings, provide training services, deliver aid, or conduct specialized research. In between are the vast majority of public policies in which eligibility and benefits are defined in terms of some kind of potentially collective, but not universal, characteristic. It is here that decisions must often be made as to *which* collective characteristics will be used as targets. Often, perceived inequality relates directly to perceived policy entitlement.

Characteristics that justify targeting can be defined in various ways. For our purposes, the primary distinction is between fundamentally *collective* criteria and other types of socio-economic criteria referring to *individual* profiles of need or deficiency. Collective characteristics (cultural, ethnic, and linguistic) are those linked in part to some kind of conscious collective identity. In some cases it is also relevant to include region of residence as a basis for such collective identity. Indeed, these geographic and cultural factors are often entwined in complex ways. Individual indicators are factors such as age, family structure, gender, income, occupation, and education. These qualities may or may not be linked to a collective identity, but they clearly represent individual-level indicators of potential need for policies of various kinds.

Underlying present discourse about group inequality in Canadian society, a distinction can also be seen between judgments of inequality based on historical conceptions of collectivist redress and those based on more contemporary indicators of resource deficiency such as income deficiency. Both of these perspectives represent an emphasis on more targeted, as opposed to universal, public policy. Collectivist redress stresses the limitations that have been imposed on particular groups because of historically stable structural aspects of a society—perhaps manifested in discrimination or prejudice. For example, this sort of reasoning has been applied to such groups as Francophones, ethnic minorities, natives, women, or residents of a particular region. Contemporary resource deficiency perspectives suggest that historical structure, although not necessarily irrelevant, is not as relevant to the design of public policy as are current indicators of individual needs and resources. The most obvious example of a response to the latter is the development of policy on the poor as defined by income deficiency.

This chapter first provides a kind of preliminary map of where Canadians generally place their preferences with respect to policy targeting techniques. Some brief attention will be given to a description of the basic pattern of perceptions. However, it is more important to consider what, if anything, is causing these attitudes. An investigation of the *determinants* of perceptions of inequality and policy entitlement will provide some insight into whether public views are grounded in a strong set of socio-economic influences, difficult to manipulate and possibly based on fairly precise assessments of policy winners and losers. If this is not the case, perhaps perceptions are largely linked to other subjective variables, more subject to manipulation and not embedded in a complex socio-economic calculus.

For our purposes, the determinants of perceived inequality fall into three general categories: subjective feelings about groups; general attitudes toward expanding state activity; and socio-economic or demographic characteristics of respondents. In this paper, it is not possible to focus directly on subjective feelings about groups, because they are not measured in the data set that is of primary interest. Thus, analysis will be concentrated on preferences for state expansion and on a very broad set of social, economic, and demographic variables. In addition to the three broad sets of influences just described, we should also note that there are historical and institutional aspects of Canadian public policy formation that will probably be important in shaping perceptions of inequality and policy entitlement. Such institutional factors cannot be treated as actual variables. Nevertheless, they may prove useful as hypothesis building and interpretative devices, and have often been used effectively in this way by scholars such as Alan Cairns (1991).

It is not difficult to appreciate that the general influences just noted might have some impact on public perceptions of group inequality. If people like a particular group (have positive feelings about it) they are more likely to feel that it experiences inequality and is entitled to public policy outputs. If people are inclined toward general expansion of state activity, they are more likely to favour increased policy activity for a variety of groups. If people have demographic or socio-economic characteristics that make it likely that they would either benefit or lose from state action pertaining to a particular group, this will likely affect their perceptions of that group's relative inequality.

Generally, it is expected that: segments of society defined in terms of non-regional characteristics will be ranked as experiencing the highest inequality and, hence, most likely in need of policy action. Such non-regional characteristics could reflect individual deficiencies such as income, but they may also reflect collective characteristics of a non-geographic nature. It is also generally expected that segments defined in terms of the oldest collective cleavages in Canadian political culture will be best explained by the array of independent variables, primarily socio-economic in nature, used in this study.

The logic behind the first point is fairly simple, and to some extent is a result of policy novelty.[2] Groups that have appeared on the policy agenda in a major way in the last three or four decades tend to be defined in terms of characteristics that are non-geographic in nature, such as the poor, women, natives, and visible minorities. As a result of the recency of their emergence as major foci for policy discourse, these groups tend to benefit from a public perception that has had less time to develop critical contours and dimensions. Whether or not these groups are objectively in need is not in question. The question is what shapes public opinion about such segments of the polity.

The logic behind the second point is similar but presented in an alternative form. Regional and linguistic groupings that have been on the policy agenda for generations have a high probability of being evaluated more critically because of the passage of large periods of time in which perceptions of such groups have been shaped. This means that groups defined by classifications based on traditional regional and linguistic cleavages will be viewed as less affected by severe inequality than are some of the newer groups involved in policy discourse. Public perceptions of the inequality and entitlement of the older objects of public policy will be lessened, because there has been a greater opportunity to translate the demands of these groups into costs and benefits for other segments of the polity. Thus, members of the public will have a more stable idea of the costs and benefits accruing to themselves as a result of policy action favourable to some established linguistic or regional grouping. The most significant expected manifestation of this linkage to a more stable predictive framework should emerge in the case of perceptions of Quebec and aspects of the Francophone community. It is anticipated that the inequality experienced by Quebec and Francophones will not be ranked highly by the public, but opinions of the public about these groups will be well anchored in basic socio-economic variables.

DATA AND METHODS

The data used in this paper are taken from the Canadian part of the 1992 International Social Survey Programme (ISSP). The weighted version of that data set used in this analysis contained 1043 weighted cases. Generally, about 750 to 850 weighted cases were usable in most parts of the analysis after cases with missing values were excluded on the basis of a listwise exclusion rule. The major variables used in the analysis of the perceived degree of policy inequality of segments of the polity are: native/aboriginal perceived inequality; women's perceived inequality; visible minorities' perceived inequality; Quebec's perceived inequality; Ontario's perceived inequality; Atlantic's perceived inequality; West's perceived inequality; Quebec Anglophones perceived inequality; Non-Quebec Francophones perceived inequality; policy entitlement of the poor.

These will be the main dependent variables in the study. For the most part, they are viewed as proxies for perceptions of the extent to which segments of society are entitled to favourable policy action to redress inequalities. It is, of course, true that one might believe that a segment or group was highly impacted by inequality but did not deserve any policy action; however, I am prepared to assume that this is unlikely to be a frequent set of attitudes.

All but one of the above variables are measured on 4-point scales with these categories: "inequality not at all serious," "inequality not very serious," "inequality somewhat serious," and "inequality very serious." The exception is the variable measuring the policy entitlement of the poor. No single question about the entitlement or inequality of the poor was directly asked in the ISSP survey. However, for purposes of comparison with other analyses, it is essential to have an indicator pertaining to the poor. For this reason, an index was constructed from four variables, each measured on a 5-point scale. These variables measured agreement with certain general opinion statements pertaining to the poor: that differences in income are too large; that government has responsibility to reduce income differences; that government should provide jobs for all willing workers; and that government should introduce a guaranteed income. This complex variable will have somewhat different, generally better, measurement properties than the other dependent variables, and will allow us to compare the poor with other groups judged to suffer from inequality in Canada.

A complex variable measuring preferences for levels of taxes or, put differently, preferences for an expansive state, was created from three questions about the appropriateness of the tax burden of different income groups. A high score on this index indicates that the respondent generally favours increases in existing tax burdens. This is used as a proxy for preferences about the expansiveness of the state. In other words, it is assumed that a person who favours higher taxes is generally favourable toward preserving or expanding the present scope of state activity.

Finally, the analysis will use standard socio-economic variables. These were selected either because they reflect whether a respondent belongs to a potentially disadvantaged group or because previous analysis has shown them to be important predictors of attitudes toward perceptions of entitlement. The variables are: gender; age; couple with children; single parent; couple without children; English mother tongue; French mother tongue; completed university degree; completed some postsecondary education; completed secondary school; self-employed; belongs to union; household income; member of management or professional class; Quebec resident; Ontario resident; Western Canada resident. It should be noted that many of the variables used above are "dummy" or dichotomous variables. Conventions for normal use of these variables dictate that one possible dichotomy will be omitted as a reference point for interpreting the other dichotomies. For example, the indicator for "Atlantic Canada Resident" is omitted to serve as a reference point for the other region of residence variables.

Considering the rather large number of variables involved, as a first step it might seem reasonable to use factor analysis to condense the dimensions of the problem. Certainly, this would be a common procedure with respect to the inequality measures used as dependent variables. In fact, some principal components analyses were run on this set of variables. Although the results were conventionally acceptable, this approach was ultimately abandoned. In the end, given the specific analytic goals of this chapter, it was decided that it would be more informative to test hypotheses using ordinary regression analysis on the original observed variables using the state expansion and socio-economic variables as predictors.

Occasional mention will be made of a similar, but not identical, analysis (Bennett, 1992) performed on a Canadian national election data set for 1988 (Northrup & Oram, 1989). Firm comparisons are not possible between the results, because somewhat different dependent and independent variables were used. The 1988 study provided indicators of perceived policy entitlement rather than of perceived inequality. It also had indicators of subjective feelings toward various polity segments that are not available in the ISSP data. The earlier study used a different segmentation of the polity, focusing less on regions than does the ISSP study. Finally, the ISSP-based analysis used region of residence as a predictor, while this was not done in the 1988 analysis. Nevertheless, there are enough conceptual linkages between the two projects to make some broad comparisons worthwhile.

RESULTS

If we look at the ten group inequality variables one by one, we can get a basic sense of how they are perceived on the average. The following shows the ranking of groups, starting with the group that is perceived as having the greatest problem of inequality and proceeding to the group with the least perceived inequality.

TABLE 1: RANKING OF GROUPS ACCORDING TO
AVERAGE PERCEIVED INEQUALITY

Group	Rank	
Natives	1	(highest perceived inequality)
Women	2	
Visible Minorities	3	
Poor	4	
English in Quebec	5	
Atlantic Canada	6	
French Outside Quebec	7	
Quebec	8	
Western Canada	9	
Ontario	10	(lowest perceived inequality)

Note, as indicated before, that the variable for the poor was based on a different measurement approach than the other variables. The ranking is based on the average agreement with the component measures used to construct the overall complex variable for the poor. This average was further adjusted to compensate for differences in the number of response categories between these variables and the other dependent variables. In the study based on 1988 data conducted by the author, the poor were ranked as the most deserving of policy action, while they are ranked fourth in this study. This may be due to differences in measurement, but other influences may be at work as well.

The findings of Table 1 are largely in accord with the expectations outlined earlier. Groups that have entered the policy agenda in a significant way in recent decades tend to be ranked relatively high in terms of their perceived inequality. Natives, women, visible minorities, and the poor occupy the top four positions in the ranking. Segments of society associated with traditional regional and/or linguistic groupings that have, in varying degrees, been a part of policy debates for generations, are ranked in the lower positions. Interestingly, Quebec and Francophones outside Quebec are not ranked at the very bottom of the list. Western Canada and Ontario hold the lowest rankings. Quite likely, this is at least partially a result of continuing perceptions that the major loci of economic strength are in the West and Ontario, and that inequality need not be addressed as a major issue for those regions.

The important point is that these rankings reflect *average* tendencies in perceived inequality. There is considerable variation around such average rankings. This leads to the primary concern of this paper. What, if anything, appears to systematically cause such variation? As illustrated in the hypotheses suggested earlier, the answers to these questions may indicate something about how perceptions of inequality and policy entitlement evolve. This, in turn, may provide us with a picture of the way in which perceived inequality and entitlement can or cannot be altered. This picture emerges in two stages—first, in the overall explanatory power of sets of variables, and, second, in a more specific consideration of individual variables.

OVERALL EXPLANATION OF PERCEIVED ENTITLEMENT

Although there is an extensive amount of information that can be extracted from the regressions, the best summary of results can probably be seen in a presentation of R-square values for the regressions. Of course, a more detailed discussion would focus on regression coefficients as well, and these will be dealt with when particularly pertinent.

Again, basic expectations outlined earlier appear to be borne out in Table 2.[3] We see that 33.6% of the variation in perceptions of inequality of Quebec and 32.3% of variation in perceptions of inequality of French outside Quebec are explained by our independent variables. After that, the explanatory power of the analysis drops dramatically, and we observe R-squares ranging from 20.5% to 16.9% for groups such as the poor, natives, Ontario, and women. A third, lower, tier of explanatory results provides R-squares ranging from 9.8% to 6.9% for segments such as Western Canada, English in Quebec, visible minorities, and Atlantic Canada.

As anticipated, regional and linguistic divisions that have existed in the Canadian polity for many years are best explained by our independent variables. The results for Quebec and the French outside Quebec stand out in this regard. More recent entrants onto the policy stage, and other regional segments, are less well explained. It is, perhaps, surprising that some of the other regions did not have higher R-squares. Certainly Atlantic Canada, Ontario, and, to a lesser degree, the West have been the subject of institutionalized policy activity for a long time. In fact, Ontario does score reasonably high, with an R-square of 18.9%. However, all of these regional segments are associated with a much lower level of explanation than are Quebec and Francophones outside that province.

TABLE 2: R-SQUARES OR PERCENTAGE VARIANCE EXPLAINED IN PERCEIVED INEQUALITY VARIABLES BY ALL EXPLANATORY VARIABLE

Dependent Variables	R-Squares
Quebec Inequality	33.6
French Outside Quebec Inequality	32.3
Poor's Inequality	20.5
Natives' Inequality	19.7
Ontario Inequality	18.9
Women's Inequality	16.9
Western Canada's Inequality	9.8
Quebec English Inequality	9.3
Visible Minority Inequality	8.6
Atlantic Canada Inequality	6.9

Part of the explanation for the regional results may be that regions outside Quebec are perceived in a less distinct fashion, and, hence, are less likely to be clearly anchored in a stable set of explanatory variables. Although objectively there may be great heterogeneity among residents of Quebec and among non-Quebec Francophones, public perception probably links them quite clearly to a limited number of cultural and linguistic characteristics as well as to distinct policy positions pertaining to the rest of Canada. Alternatively, Ontario, Atlantic Canada, and the West can be more easily perceived in terms of a wide variety of linguistic and cultural traits as well as tremendous variation in socio-economic profiles.

IMPACTS OF SPECIFIC VARIABLES

Thus far, we have been examining how total variation in perceived entitlement of groups can be accounted for by general blocks of independent variables. There are, however, important issues that can only be addressed by looking at the impact of independent variables in a regression separately. This involves looking at specific regression coefficients.

Some very schematic information on regression coefficients in ten regressions is provided in Tables 3a and 3b. The first provides results for the five groups that had the highest R-squares in results already presented—Quebec, Francophones outside Quebec, the poor, natives, and Ontario. Table 3b presents similar results for the groups associated with lower R-squares—women, Western Canada, English in Quebec, visible minorities, and Atlantic Canada. For any variable that had a significant (.05 or lower) impact, the Beta (standardized coefficient) is reported. In instances where a variable was close to significance (.05 to .1 range) and might well be conventionally significant were other weak variables dropped from the regression, the Beta is provided within parentheses.

The most important pieces of information in these tables are the signs of the coefficients. However, Beta values are provided in order to approximate standard expectations for reporting of results. Beta coefficients are reported here rather than unstandardized coefficients because they give an approximate picture of the relative importance of variables in the same equation.

Turning first to the *level of taxation preference* variable, we see very limited significant impacts. In two cases, the poor and women, this independent variable had a significant positive effect. In other words, those who favoured higher taxes tended to see inequality as a relatively important problem for the poor and women. Basically, people who saw inequality for these groups as a problem were willing to raise taxes to alleviate it. This can be understood in terms of the obvious linkage of the poor and, to a lesser extent, women to problems that could be addressed to some extent through income redistribution. There is also a weak negative impact of the tax preference variable on perceptions of the inequality of English in Quebec. Possibly respondents felt that English Quebecers still occupied a particularly privileged position in that province. However, this picture of English Quebec is probably not as accurate today as it might have been some generations ago.[4]

TABLE 3A: REGRESSION PREDICTORS OF PERCEIVED INEQUALITIES

Groups Perceived in Terms of Inequality

Independent Variables	Quebec	French Outside Quebec	Poor	Natives	Ontario
Tax Preference Variable			.088		
Gender	-.144	-.140	-.196	-.112	-.090
Age	-.113	(-.067)			
Couple With Children	.083				
Single Parent			(.060)		
Couple Without Children					
English Mother Tongue		(.122)			
French Mother Tongue	.213	.203		(-.143)	
Completed University	-.158	.175	-.237	.207	-.304
Postsecondary Education	-.174		-.317		-.215
Completed Secondary School	-.156		-.184		(-.099)
Self-Employed					
Union Member			.148		
Manager					.081
Household Income	-.123		-.211		-.157
Quebec Resident	.232	.362			(.150)
Ontario Resident				.147	
Western Canada Resident		-.121		(.122)	(-.123)

Note: Beta coefficients significant at .10 or less are reported. Those significant between .05 and .1 are given in parentheses.

TABLE 3B: REGRESSION PREDICTORS OF PERCEIVED INEQUALITIES

Groups Perceived in Terms of Inequality

Independent Variables	Women	Western Canada	English in Quebec	Visible Minorities	Atlantic Canada
Tax Preference Variable	.077		(-.074)		
Gender	-.342			-.203	-.121
Age				-.090	.117
Couple With Children					
Single Parent				(.069)	
Couple Without Children	.100				
English Mother Tongue				(.125)	(.139)
French Mother Tongue			-.175		
Completed University					
Some Postsecondary Education	-.209	(-.121)			
Completed Secondary School	-.191				
Self-Employed	(.067)				
Union Member					
Manager		(.076)			
Household Income		-.160	-.098	-.104	
Quebec Resident	(.140)			(.160)	
Ontario Resident	(.123)				-.163
Western Canada Resident	(.124)	.184			(-.131)

Note: Beta coefficients significant at .10 or less are reported. Those significant between .05 and .1 are given in parentheses.

The independent variable *household income* had a significant negative impact in six instances, on perceptions of inequality pertaining to Quebec, the poor, Ontario, Western Canada, English in Quebec, and visible minorities. This result is not difficult to understand, as people with high incomes may be expected to be sceptical of claims to inequality of a wide variety of groups, because efforts to offset such inequality might place greater pressure on taxes for those with middle to high incomes. Keeping in mind that variables and variable definitions were somewhat different, analysis of 1988 data showed similar wide-ranging negative income effects.

Independent variables pertaining to *level of education* were often significant. The dummy variables relating to completion of university, some postsecondary education, and completion of secondary education are measured relative to the excluded low education group, which had not completed secondary school. The completion of university variable had three significant negative impacts (Quebec, poor, and Ontario) and two significant positive impacts (French outside Quebec and natives). The completed some postsecondary education variable also had three significant negative impacts on perceptions of inequality for Quebec, the poor, and Ontario, as well as a negative impact on perceptions of inequality for women and a marginally negative impact on perceptions of inequality for Western Canada. The completed secondary school variables had negative impacts on perceived inequality of Quebec, the poor, Ontario (marginally significant), and women.

The influence of education is not totally surprising. Education is often an important predictor of response on opinion and preference variables. This is partly the case for methodological reasons; people who are more educated tend to interpret questions differently from less educated ones. However, there are also substantive reasons why education can be expected to impact on the kinds of dependent variables of interest here. This result can be best understood against the background of the prevalence of negative signs for the education variables. These signs mean that, in general, people who are more educated (those who have at least completed secondary school) are less likely to perceive problems of inequality for certain groups than are less educated people (those without secondary school completion). This pattern was also apparent in an analysis of 1988 Canadian data. In fact, the pattern of negative results was even more marked in the earlier data set. It suggests that more educated Canadians are taking a relatively critical and analytically discriminating view of claims of perceived inequality and entitlement. More educated Canadians may be cautious in assigning markers of need to certain groups because they understand the possible link that such perceptions may have to the design of public policy—policy that may not always be carefully defined. Although raw education and income variables are correlated, the phenomenon of the negative education impacts is not another income effect, because the effects of income and education are separated in the regression. However, education may also have a link to future expectations of income and the policy context of such expectations. By way of qualification, it is worth noting that within the set of people who had at least completed secondary school, one does find more positive impacts of education on perceived inequality at the top of the educated group—those with university degrees. Thus, at the very high end of the education spectrum, the negatively critical perspective taken on the inequality problems is slightly reduced in prevalence, but negative signs still predominate.

Other variables that are particularly noteworthy in terms of statistical significance are *gender* and *age*. This is particularly important in that these variables were of little importance in the analysis of 1988 data. Thus, despite cautions relating to differences in variables and data sets, these results may signal a crystallization of some new demographic constraints on perceptions of inequality. Looking first at the gender variable, it had a significant negative impact on perceived inequality of eight groups. It was without significant impact only in the case of Western Canada and English in Quebec. Giving the mechanics of coding of the gender variable, this means that men consistently perceived inequality to be less of a problem than did women. This result is not due to the crude fact that men tend to have higher incomes than women. One must remember that regression partials out the influence of one independent variable (such as income) from another (such as gender). We are probably witnessing something more complex here. It may, to some degree, be policy-induced, since men as a segment of the polity have been increasingly excluded from initiatives relating to equity and redistribution.

Age had a significant negative impact on perceptions of Quebec inequality, a marginally significant negative impact on perceptions relating to French outside Quebec, a significant negative impact on perceptions pertaining to visible minorities, and a positive impact on perceptions of inequality for Atlantic Canada. Older people had a moderate tendency to give low estimations of inequality as a problem. One can speculate that this may have something to do with older people's concerns for their own security as a segment of the polity, and their anxiety over other groups crowding the policy agenda. It may also simply be the result of generational differences in experience of and exposure to policy concerns.

Another finding to underline here is the influence of the *mother tongue* variables. In analysis of 1988 data, French mother tongue status often had a positive influence on perceptions of the entitlement of various groups. In the current data set, we see that only two clear positive effects are shown—one on perceptions of inequality for Quebec and the other on perceptions of inequality for French outside Quebec. Again, precise comparisons are not possible, because of the conceptual and measurement differences between variables, but there is at least the hint of a change in the influence of mother tongue. In addition to the positive effects noted, there is a marginal negative impact on perceptions of natives and a significant negative impact on perceptions of Quebec English inequality.

One of the probable reasons for the difference between the current results and those in the 1988 study is to be found in the fact that the current analysis untangles the effects of language and *region*. This was not true in the earlier study. Thus, some of the impacts associated with mother tongue in the 1988 data are more clearly associated with a particular region. Indeed, in the current study, residency in Quebec has taken over some of the widespread positive influence that had previously been associated with French mother tongue. Quebec residency has positive impacts on perceived inequality for Quebec and non-Quebec Francophones as well as marginal positive impacts on perceptions of inequality for Ontario, women and visible minorities.[5]

What of the relative sizes of the Beta estimates? Do they provide additional noteworthy information? At one level, they tend to be consistent with what one would expect from simple self-interest and personal identity explanations of perceptions. For example, French mother tongue and Quebec residency are the largest estimated impacts on perceptions of inequality for Quebec, non-Quebec Francophones, and Quebec Anglophones. Similarly, the largest Beta in the perception of Western inequality equation is Western residence status. In the same vein, gender has the largest impact by far in the equation for perceptions of women's inequality. In contrast to this, Ontario residence status does not have a significant impact of any magnitude on perceptions of Ontario inequality, a testimony to the diversity associated with that province.

Apart from these not unexpected results, one does observe a major role for education and, to a lesser extent, income variables. They are associated with the largest estimated impacts for perceptions of the poor, natives, and Ontario. One or more of these variables plays a substantial but secondary role in the equations for Quebec, non-Quebec Francophones, women, and Western Canada.

In the equations with smaller R-squares, we do see a couple of less expected but not totally surprising results. Gender has the largest absolute impact on perceptions of visible minorities. This can be explained in terms of the field of conflict defined by equity policies and the emerging crystallization of male, particularly white male, opinions on equity policies. Quite likely, if the data set contained a country of birth or ethnicity variable, it would rival the influence of gender in this equation. By a small margin, Ontario residence status has the largest impact on the perceptions of Atlantic Canada. Perhaps, in a small way, the negative sign of this relationship reflects a growing intolerance toward interregional equalization at a time when Ontario has also experienced structural economic shocks. However, as suggested before, one must be careful not to make too much of sample estimates of Beta magnitudes.

Two primary expectations noted at the beginning of this analysis have, for the most part, been borne out. First, it was expected that segments of society defined in terms of non-regional characteristics would have higher perceived inequality than regionally and geographically defined segments or geographically concentrated, traditional linguistic segments. This was clearly shown to be the case in Table 1. Second, it was anticipated that those segments that are redolent of the oldest cleavages in the Canadian polity would be best explained by the wide array of independent variables utilized in the study. This also proved to be generally true, in that variance in perceptions of inequality for Quebec and for French outside of Quebec were best explained by the regressions that were tested in Table 2. These findings tend to support what might be termed a policy novelty perspective on perceptions of entitlement, need, and inequality. The term "novelty" is not used in a pejorative sense. It simply suggests that it takes time for perceptions to become well grounded in socio-economic and demographic predictors. It is also true that differences in results for regionally vs. non-regionally defined segments are due to the fact that there is generally greater socio-economic heterogeneity within regions than within other types of polity segments.

Substantial results pertaining to the influence of specific independent variables were also displayed in Tables 3a and 3b. Although we did not outline expectations for individual impacts, the results for specific independent variables do seem to follow some discernible patterns. For example, income, education, gender, and age tended to be important. In general, and there are exceptions to this, higher income people, more educated people, men, and older people tended to have lower perceptions of inequality as a problem for various segments of the polity. Some of these findings are attributable to simple conceptions of self-interest. Others may signal shifts in the policy-relevant contours of public opinion.

As has been suggested several times, there are some interesting comparisons to be made between these findings for the 1992 International Social Survey Programme and earlier findings based on a 1988 Canadian national election data set, but comparisons must be treated with caution, since the two analyses differed in the way segments of the polity were defined, in terms of independent variables used, and in terms of somewhat different conceptualizations of perceived need. The earlier study focused on entitlement to policy action and the later on perceived inequality. It appears that gender and age emerge as more important influences in the ISSP data, and income and education are important in both sets of data. It is also noteworthy that socio-economic variables seemed to be more potent in the ISSP analysis than in the earlier analysis. However, this may have something to do with the fact that the earlier analysis was able to use subjective feelings about groups as entitlement predictors, and part of the influence of such variables would remain entwined with the socio-economic variables in the ISSP study. Nevertheless, socio-economic variables do seem to play a more powerful role in explaining 1992 perceptions of inequality than in explaining 1988 perceptions of entitlement.

One of the primary motivations for this analysis was to begin to map Canadian perceptions of need for state action, policy entitlement, and attention to inequality, and the determinants of such perceptions. What begins to emerge is the possibility that recency of introduction to the organized policy agenda may be crudely associated with perceived entitlement. Yet, citizens may often have a limited basis for linking these perceptions to any detailed socio-economic indicators of group interest and citizen interest until some time has passed. Perceptions of groups may become less charitable as time passes, simply because they are placed in a much richer context of objective indicators of need and interest.

In my view, this creates certain inefficiencies in the life of democracies. One of the springs of this inefficiency is that policy is often defined in terms of highly aggregated or collective targets. At least, this may be true of the policies that enter into the realm of public discourse. What is the alternative? The alternative might be a more conscious attempt to discuss entitlement in terms of multi-dimensional profiles of individual need. The beginning of any policy discourse should be an attempt to structure discussion in terms of micro-variation in individual needs and profiles rather than in terms of gross, one-dimensional characterizations by a single indicator, such as age, gender, race, ethnicity, income, region of residence, language, family type, or sexual orientation. One of the interesting implications of a more fine-grained and multi-dimensional discussion of entitlement would be a rethinking of the place of historical redress in policy debates. No collectivity consists of a single history, nor does it have a single history in relation to other collectivities. Rather, it consists of multitudes of individuals, each with distinct histories, needs, and potential claims.

The primary reason why a more nuanced approach to defining entitlement to policy would have a slow birth is that political leadership and political institutions would have to work much harder to create committed audiences and to package highly varied policies. In addition, policy discussion phrased in terms of the real complexities of individuals would make it far more difficult for politicians and bureaucrats to create the caricatures and illusions that further their own careers as opposed to some broader, perhaps public, interest.

What would the future of public policy be if the rather "lumpy" characteristics of its current design, packaging, and delivery were modified? Can the mass citizenry as well as elites be trained to think in terms of complex indicators of individual need rather than cultural collectivities or similarly diverse groups? These are useful questions, even if one believes that there are types of collectivities in which individual circumstances are unavoidably constrained.

There could be two effects of defining policy to a greater extent in terms of individual needs. First, such an approach could be associated with a greater universality of policy, in the sense that minimum standards would be ensured for everyone and deficiencies addressed on an individual basis relative to a common standard. Second, policy might be increasingly concentrated in areas where there was strong agreement that universal standards were possible. Where such agreement did not exist, solutions would be sought in private arrangements or non-governmental collectivities. Some of these collectivities might be based on cultural or linguistic groupings, but I expect that communities based on commonality of value systems might become just as important.

An alternative scenario might involve policy having a higher degree of socio-economic targeting in conjunction with a patch work approach of different policy packages for different socio-economic groups. However, this is only likely if institutional constraints on policy design evolved in a manner that encouraged elites and the public to think in a much more technically informed manner about policy in general. In any event, there is room for reconsidering the way that policy entitlement is defined and discussed. It may be possible to do this without limiting the content of policy to process questions. It cannot be done without some greater examination of individual, as opposed to collective, variation in entitlement.

ENDNOTES

1. In recent years, some of the commentary on groups seeking legitimacy and representation has been couched in phrases such as the "politics of recognition" or the "politics of identity." See for example, the very skilful probing of this area against the backdrop of communitarian and libertarian debates in Charles Taylor, "The Politics of Recognition," in Amy Gutmann, ed., *Multiculturalism: Examining the Politics of Recognition*, (Princeton, 1994), pp. 25-74. I would simply note that calculation and self-interest over time offer another portal for viewing this drama. Indeed, if one can discuss the instrumental orientation of nationalist movements in other parts of the world, we cannot assume that our own politics of recognition is without its instrumental side.

2. A recent reading of a student paper reminded me that the logic of this policy novelty perspective shares some of the same foundations as Anthony Downs' theory of issue cycles discussed in Anthony Downs, "Up and Down with Ecology: The 'Issue Attention Cycle,'" *The Public Interest, 28* (Spring, 1972), 38-50. The present work focuses on policy-relevant perceptions of groups rather than issues. However, the idea that there may be phases during which people become increasingly aware of costs and benefits associated with policy has general applicability. When the objects of attention are groups, the phases may be very long.

3. All of the R-squares in Table 2 are significant at .05 or less due to large sample size. The precise significance levels are probably slightly distorted due to non-normality in some of the error distributions. Again, due to sample size the distortions are

probably minor. The author is well aware of criticisms directed at the use of correlations as indicators. However, as a summary device they are useful and are not problematic for our immediate purpose, since we are not comparing across samples.

4. Generally, the comparable taxation preference/state expansion variable in an analysis of 1988 data was more likely to be significant. However, the variable was not exactly the same as the variable constructed for this study and was applied with a somewhat different set of dependent and independent variables.

5. The Cairns work noted earlier is also suggestive of the crowding of the constitutional policy agenda in recent years and how that may have forced a different set of perceptions and interests in French speakers, particularly in Quebec.

REFERENCES

Bennett, Scott. (1992). Public Perceptions of Collective Entitlement: Segmented Views of Policy in Canadian Democracy. A paper presented at the Conference on Democratic Politics at Carleton University in Ottawa, Canada, in November, 1992.

Cairns, Alan C. (1991). Author's Introduction: The Growth of Constitutional Self-Consciousness. In D. E. Williams (Ed.), *Disruptions: Constitutional Struggles from the Charter to Meech Lake* (pp. 13-33). Toronto: McClelland & Stewart.

Downs, Anthony. (1972). Up and Down with Ecology: The Issue Attention Cycle. *The Public Interest, 28*, 38-50.

Northrup, D., & Oram, A. (1989). *The 1988 National Election Study: Technical Documentation*. North York, Ontario: York University, Institute for Social Research.

Taylor, Charles. (1994). The Politics of Recognition. In A. Gutmann (Ed.), *Multiculturalism: Examining the Politics of Recognition* (pp. 25-73). Princeton: Princeton University Press.

CHAPTER SIX

LANGUAGE, REGION, RACE, GENDER, AND INCOME: PERCEPTIONS OF INEQUALITIES IN QUEBEC AND ENGLISH CANADA

Leslie S. Laczko

CANADA IS AN ADVANCED industrial society with extensive class cleavages. According to most widely used indicators of class inequality, such as wealth and income, Canada's level of class inequality is comparable to that found in most industrial societies (see chapter 2 of this volume). At the same time, the ideological view that Canada is a relatively open and class-less society is widespread (see chapter 4 of this volume). The well established objective inequalities are not accompanied by a strong sense of class consciousness and class voting (see Pammett, 1987). On most measures of these two dimensions, Canada's international position is widely judged to be low (Goyder, 1990, 182).

Canada is also characterized by a high degree of regionalism and a complex pattern of ethnic and linguistic diversity, or pluralism, both of which are mediated through a federal political system. In Canada's federal system the power of the provinces is appreciable, even compared to the power of provinces and states in other decentralized federations. Also, Canada's overall level of ethnic and linguistic diversity is quite high compared to that of other highly developed societies. This is because Canada combines different types of ethnic and linguistic differentiation within a single society and political system. Canada's historic French-English dualism has led to two sets of parallel institutions divided along linguistic lines. This is a feature that Canada shares with Belgium and Switzerland.

At the same time, Canada is a new world society in which aboriginal peoples have become subordinate minorities, and in which successive waves of immigrants have also been been incorporated into the larger society. This is a feature that Canada shares with Australia, New Zealand, and the United States (Laczko, 1994).

Within this complex plural structure, a total picture includes inequalities as well. In addition to the inequalities between social classes found in all industrial societies, Canada also displays inequalities between several status and power groups. There are inequalities between regions, between language groups, between native or aboriginal populations and the larger society, between men and women, and between the recently recognized category of visible minorities and the larger society. This chapter investigates how some of these group and class inequalities were perceived by the Canadian population in 1992. Special attention will be paid to the different outlooks displayed by respondents in Quebec and in the rest of Canada.

In recent decades, prevailing societal definitions of what constitutes relevant and important group inequalities have been changing in Canada, as well as in other industrial societies. While some types of cleavage have been an enduring part of the landscape, others are more recent in their arrival in the political arena. We shall be examining both older and newer types of group inequality.

Inequalities between wealthier and poorer regions have been a central issue in Canadian society and politics throughout Canadian history. Since the passage of the Official Languages Act in 1969, it has become customary to refer to two official language minorities, namely Francophones outside Quebec and Anglophones in Quebec. Since the 1980s, native and aboriginal issues have come "out of irrelevance" (Ponting & Gibbins, 1980) to occupy a more central place on the political agenda at the national level. Also, the multiculturalism and employment programs of both the federal and provincial governments have become increasingly focused on providing equal access to members of a new and emerging legal category of "visible minority." At the same time, women's issues have become politicized more than ever before. The politicization of both older and newer types of groups has been facilitated and encouraged by the Canadian Charter of Rights and Freedoms, enacted in 1982, and further crystallized during the lengthy negotiations over the failed Meech Lake Accord (1987-1990) and the Charlottetown Agreement, defeated by referendum in October 1992. The arrival on the national political scene of a number of newer types of status groups has been traced to the actions of the state in funding these interest groups. Increasingly in recent decades, the state has been involved in defining and shaping the organizations that "represent" group constituencies (Cairns, 1986; Pal, 1993).

An examination of possibly distinct patterns of responses in Quebec is justified on several grounds. Quebec's history is at the origin of Canada's high level of pluralism, and intergroup relations in Quebec display their own complex dynamics in ways that often set Quebec off from the rest of Canada. As a setting where both French and English majority cultures and institutions have long co-existed side by side and in competition with each other, Quebec's Francophone majority and Anglophone minority both exhibit a mix of majority and minority characteristics. Recent decades in Quebec have been marked by several waves of legislation aimed at reducing long-standing inequalities in the province, in the context of competing state- and nation-building programs carried out by the Quebec and federal governments. The recent rounds of constitutional negotiations have shown that accommodating the special interests of Quebec in a way that gains the consensus of aboriginal peoples, the other provinces, Francophones outside Quebec, and Anglophones in Quebec, as well as other organized interest groups, is proving a very difficult task. It has been argued that minorities are often more aware of all aspects of a power relationship. Following this logic, we might expect Quebec respondents in 1992 to display a higher level of awareness of group inequalities, and also perhaps a higher level of concern for income and class inequalities, and a higher level of support for state activity to reduce inequalities.

The 1992 Canadian ISSP Survey contains measures of perceptions of both status/power group inequalities and class inequalities. With respect to group inequalities, measures are available of the perceived extent to which inequalities are experienced by natives, women, visible minorities, and official language minorities, as well as by Quebec, Atlantic Canada, Ontario, and the West (see chapter 5). These provide an opportunity to analyze group inequalities with data based on survey questions never before asked in Canada. The ISSP data set also contains, in a somewhat different format, a set of questions dealing with perceptions of income inequality and orientations toward state intervention aimed at reducing it. Both of these sets of questions will be examined here, with special attention being paid to the distinct pattern of responses in Quebec. The chapter will go on to consider perceived status group inequalities, perceived class inequalities, and the linkages between these two sets of perceptions.

PERCEPTIONS OF GROUP INEQUALITY: HOW MANY DIMENSIONS ARE THERE?

The extent to which certain status/power groups in Canadian society are perceived as experiencing inequality is tapped by a set of measures with the following format. Respondents were asked:

It has been suggested that some specific groups or regions are not treated equally in Canadian society. How seriously would you say the following suffer from inequality? (please tick one box on each line)

For each named region or group, the choices available are "not at all serious," "not very serious," "somewhat serious," and "very serious."

TABLE 1: FACTOR ANALYSIS OF 9 MEASURES OF
PERCEIVED SERIOUSNESS OF GROUP INEQUALITY, CANADA, 1992

	I Quebec/ Francophones	II Minorities and women	III English regions
Inequality experienced by ...			
Aboriginals/Natives	-.26	.79	.19
Women	.41	.70	.05
Visible Minorities	.21	.79	.04
Quebec	.88	.10	.03
Ontario	.59	-.08	.49
Atlantic Canada	.32	.25	.64
The West	.27	-.02	.75
Anglophones in Quebec	-.16	.13	.71
Francophones outside Quebec	.73	.16	.14
Eigenvalue	3.02	1.52	1.24
% of total variance	33.5	16.9	13.8

The list of nine regional and group labels is shown on the left side of Table 1. This list includes four regions of Canada, two official language minorities, and three "newer" or more recently politicized minorities. How are these nine measures related to each other? The vast majority of the pairwise bivariate correlations between the measures are positive (not shown). Beyond this, are the nine measures reducible to a smaller number of dimensions? Table 1 presents the results of a principal components factor analysis of these nine variables. As can be seen from the factor loadings in each column, the data do reveal an underlying structure that is represented here by the first three principal components. These three are the only ones that have eigenvalues greater than 1. Since the analysis was carried out using a varimax rotation, the three factors are independent of each other.

The first of these, represented by the column of data on the left-hand side, can be interpreted as representing Quebec and Francophone concerns, since the two variables that load most highly on this factor are those asking about Quebec and Francophones outside Quebec. We might note the negative loadings on this factor of the questions dealing with aboriginals and Anglophones in Quebec, indicating a source of tension or antipathy to which we shall be returning. At the same time, the question about Ontario inequality also loads moderately highly on this factor, suggesting that to some extent this factor is measuring opinions about the relative position of central Canada, and not just Quebec.

The second principal component, represented by the middle column, can be interpreted as tapping concern with the position of the newer, more recently politicized minorities, namely aboriginals, women, and visible minorities. The third factor, on the right hand side, taps the position of the regions of the country other than Quebec. Interestingly, the question dealing with Anglophones in Quebec loads highly on this factor, suggesting that in popular perceptions Anglophones in Quebec are an English-speaking region of Canada rather than a minority group. This is certainly consonant with Anglophone Quebecers' self-definition for much of Canadian history. The position of this group has been changing, of course, and its location in the public mind is complex, as we shall see shortly.

How can we measure the population's relative assessment of the different types of regional and group inequalities? The data at hand allow us to approach this question in two ways. First, since all of the questions were asked using the same format and question wording, we can compare the central tendencies of the nine questionnaire items. Table 2 shows the mean values of each of the measures, among respondents in Quebec and in the rest of Canada.

The first point to mention about Table 2 is that the average scores tend to be higher in Quebec than in the rest of Canada. This tendency of Quebec respondents to view many types of group inequality as being more serious than do respondents elsewhere in Canada is marked by a few exceptions, however. These exceptions concern responses dealing with aboriginal inequality and inequality experienced by Anglophones in

Quebec, both of which are judged to be significantly less serious by Quebecers than by residents of the other provinces. At the same time, the inequalities suffered by Quebec and by Francophones outside Quebec are judged to be *much* more serious by Quebec respondents than by others. These significant divergences in outlook lead to a rather different set of rank orderings in Quebec and in the rest of Canada. The Spearman's rho rank-order correlation coefficient of .35 indicates that the two rank orderings, while in the same overall direction, do display important divergences with respect to the four group labels just mentioned. At the same time, it is interesting to note the general agreement between Quebec and the rest of Canada with respect to inequalities experienced by women, visible minorities, and the other regions. Both in Quebec and elsewhere, Ontario is judged to suffer the least from inequality.

The second approach to assessing which types of inequality are seen as most serious is to ask respondents about the issue directly. Replies to such a direct question, about the single most urgent type of group inequality in need of attention, are shown in Table 3. The picture that emerges is similar to that already seen in Table 2. Quebec respondents are much more likely to assign top priority to Quebec and to Francophones outside Quebec, and a lower priority to aboriginal inequality.

The pattern observed so far points to the centrality of the long-standing linguistic and cultural cleavage between Quebec and the rest of Canada, with a newer twist to it, in the form of lukewarm feelings toward aboriginal issues in Quebec and a much more positive disposition toward native inequality and native issues elsewhere in Canada. This reflects the ongoing constitutional disputes of the late 1980s and early 1990s, as well as the fallout from the Oka crisis of 1990. We shall be returning to the way the Quebec and native issues are linked shortly.

Another major difference revealed by Table 3 is that in the collective mind of Canada outside Quebec, Anglophone Quebecers appear to suffer from more inequality than either Quebec as a whole or than Francophones outside Quebec. This is consonant with the results of Table 2. Canadians outside Quebec may well assign a low priority to the inequality suffered by Quebec partly because Quebec is seen as part of a powerful central Canada, as already seen in Table 1. Also, Table 3 shows that in the collective mind of Quebecers, the inequality suffered by Francophones outside Quebec is assigned a low priority, even though Quebecers judge this type of inequality to be the most serious of all in Table 2. This disjunction reflects the tensions in Canada's federal system between

TABLE 2: PERCEIVED SERIOUSNESS OF VARIOUS GROUP INEQUALITIES, QUEBEC AND REST OF CANADA, 1992

	Rest of Canada		Quebec	
	Mean Value	Rank Order	Mean Value	Rank Order
Inequality experienced by ...				
Aboriginals/Natives	3.34	1	2.69	5
Women	2.82	2	3.06	2
Visible Minorities	2.82	3	2.82	4
Quebec	1.84	8	3.00	3
Ontario	1.48	9	1.95	9
Atlantic Canada	2.38	5	2.63	6
The West	1.95	7	2.04	8
Anglophones in Quebec	2.67	4	2.27	7
Francophones outside Quebec	2.10	6	3.12	1

Entries are mean values with 1 = not at all serious, 4 = very serious.
Number of cases (range): Canada outside Quebec (666-688).
  Quebec (217-232).

Spearman's rho = .35

TABLE 3: SINGLE MOST SERIOUS TYPE OF GROUP INEQUALITY, QUEBEC AND REST OF CANADA, 1992

"If you think that some groups are not treated equally, what group or region do you consider constitutes the top priority for action to change the situation?"

	Rest of Canada	Quebec
Natives/Aboriginals	50.1%	10.4%
Women	20.6	32.2
Visible Minorities	6.0	7.9
Quebec	3.4	28.6
Ontario	1.5	—
Atlantic Canada	4.9	0.6
The West	1.9	—
Anglophones in Quebec	4.8	1.9
Francophones outside Quebec	0.1	7.5
No Inequality	3.3	6.5
Refused	0.6	0.3
Don't Know	2.9	3.8
	100.1	99.9
Number of cases	(699)	(242)

Percentages do not total 100 exactly because of rounding.

linguistic majorities and minorities, and in particular the complex ways in which the interests of Francophones in Quebec and in the rest of Canada overlap in some ways, and diverge in other ways. Put differently, Quebecers are the most aware of the inequality suffered by Francophones outside Quebec, and they judge it to be more serious than other types of group inequality. At the same time, this level of awareness does not lead Quebecers to grant this type of inequality a very high priority.

VARIATIONS IN CONSENSUS ABOUT
TYPES OF GROUP INEQUALITY

The different types of inequalities do not all elicit the same degree of consensus regarding their relative seriousness. These variations, and the different patterns found in Quebec and elsewhere in the country, are illustrated in Table 4, which gives measures of ambivalence and of consensus concerning the seriousness of various inequalities.

Panel A of the table reveals yet another difference between respondents in Quebec and those in the rest of Canada. On average, Quebec respondents are more likely to give don't know answers to this series of questions, possibly suggesting a greater ambivalence. In panel B, two ways of representing variation about the mean seriousness values are shown, and each can provide useful information. The standard deviations (SD) measure internal disagreement and lack of consensus. Almost all the standard deviations are higher in Quebec than in the rest of Canada, suggesting that in Quebec there exists more internal debate and less internal consensus on these issues. Beyond this, the main foci of ambivalence are not identical in Quebec and in English Canada. Quebec respondents show the least consensus concerning inequalities experienced by natives, and by Anglophones in Quebec, in part reflecting the different outlooks of the Francophone majority and the Anglophone and other minorities within Quebec on these two questions. In the rest of Canada, respondents display the least consensus with respect to inequalities experienced by Anglophones in Quebec. This possibly reflects both the historic role of English-speaking Quebec as a Canada-wide dominant group, as opposed to its other role as an official language minority on the same legal and symbolic footing as Francophones outside Quebec. This ambivalent and complex view of Anglophone Quebec is one that both Quebec and the rest of Canada have in common.

The coefficient of variation (CV) adjusts each standard deviation for differences in magnitude of the means. The degree of dispersion of each

TABLE 4: MEASURES OF AMBIVALENCE AND CONSENSUS IN
PERCEIVED SERIOUSNESS OF GROUP INEQUALITIES, 1992

	Rest of Canada		Quebec	
A				
Percent with one or more "don't know" answers to 9 questions about inequalities	7%		14%	
Mean number of "don't know" answers	.29		.61	
B	SD	CV	SD	CV
Indices of dispersion[1] of measures of perceived seriousness of inequality experienced by				
Aboriginals/Natives	.79	.24	1.04	.39
Women	.83	.30	.89	.29
Visible Minorities	.82	.29	.80	.28
Quebec	.89	.48	.94	.31
Ontario	.70	.47	.91	.47
Atlantic Canada	.92	.39	.94	.36
The West	.86	.44	.87	.43
Anglophones in Quebec	.95	.36	1.06	.47
Francophones outside Quebec	.78	.37	.91	.29

1. SD is the standard deviation of each score. The lower the standard deviation, the greater the consensus.
    CV is the coefficient of variation of each score. This is the standard deviation divided by the mean, which was given in Table 2. The lower the coefficient of variation, the greater the relative consensus.

measure relative to its mean value can be interpreted as a degree of relative consensus of opinion on the issue. If we compare the columns of CVs in Quebec and the rest of Canada, it is clear that most are quite similar, with a few exceptions. The exceptions reveal yet another aspect of the cleavage pattern already seen. The questions about the inequality experienced by natives and by Anglophones in Quebec display much higher CVs in Quebec than in the rest of Canada, while the questions about the inequality experienced by Quebec and by Francophones outside Quebec display much lower CVs in Quebec than in the rest of Canada. Thus, Quebec displays relatively more internal disagreement concerning the inequalities experienced by aboriginals and Quebec Anglophones, and less internal disagreement concerning the inequalities experienced by Quebec and by Francophones outside Quebec.[1]

INCOME INEQUALITY AND STATE INTERVENTION

We now turn to measures that tap inequalities between social classes. These are questions that ask about perceived income inequality and about state intervention to reduce income inequality and provide employment. The exact wording of these questions is shown in Table 5 (see also chapter 4).

TABLE 5: PERCEIVED INCOME INEQUALITY AND OPINIONS
ON STATE INTERVENTION, 1992

	Rest of Canada	Quebec	
	Mean (s.d)	Mean (s.d.)	(t-value)
A "Differences in income in Canada are too large"	3.74 (1.00)	4.02 (.95)	(3.76)
B "It is the responsibility of the government to reduce the differences in income between people with high incomes and those with low incomes"	3.16 (1.22)	3.50 (1.26)	(3.56)
"The government should provide a job for everyone who wants one"	2.87 (1.24)	3.56 (1.17)	(7.49)
"The government should provide everyone with a guaranteed basic income"	3.10 (1.30)	3.47 (1.31)	(3.80)

Mean values on a 5 point scale, with 1= strongly disagree, 5= strongly agree.
Number of cases (range): Quebec (229-238);
Rest of Canada (669-682).

Let us focus first on the mean values reported in the table. As can be seen in panel A, Quebec respondents are significantly more likely than respondents elsewhere in Canada to agree with a statement that income differences in Canada are too large. The results of panel B show that, in similar fashion, Quebec respondents are more likely to agree that it is the government's role to reduce income inequalities, that government should provide jobs, and that government should provide a basic income. The right-hand side of the table displays the values of the t-statistic, the ratio of each mean to its standard error. All of the t-values are well above 2.0, indicating that these differences are statistically significant and much larger than any differences that might be due to sampling error.

Further information can be gleaned from the standard deviations that appear in parentheses below each mean value. In this series the Quebec standard deviations are not appreciably different from those elsewhere in Canada, unlike the earlier questions dealing with regional and group inequalities. Also, it is noteworthy that both in Quebec and elsewhere, the standard deviation in panel A is lower than those in panel B. This means that there is more of a consensus about assessments of whether income differences are too large than there is about the various state intervention measures.

CLASS INEQUALITY AND GROUP INEQUALITY

In the preceding sections we examined various measures of group inequality and class inequality, and saw that, in this 1992 sample, Quebecers are more likely than other Canadians to see both as serious. Are the two sets of measures close enough to allow an answer to the question of which of the two types is judged to be the more serious type by the Canadian population? A direct comparison of central tendencies is not possible, since the two sets of measures use different formats—a four-point scale in one set, a five-point scale in the other—as well as different question wordings. For this reason, less direct methods of assessing the relative importance of the two types of perceptions must be used. In chapter 5 of this volume, Scott Bennett applies a statistical adjustment to the scales, which yields the result that income inequality (in Bennett's terms, the inequality suffered by a group, the poor) is ranked as among the more serious types of inequality that respondents were asked to assess.

Another related aspect of the way the two types of perceptions are related is provided by factor analysis. Interesting results are obtained if, for heuristic purposes, we disregard the differences in format between the two sets of measures, and combine the two sets into an enhanced matrix of thirteen variables, composed of the nine group inequality measures and the four class (or, more specifically, income inequality and state intervention) measures. If this enlarged set of thirteen variables is subjected to a factor analysis, then the four income inequality measures do load highly on a distinct principal component, as can be seen from Table 6.

Table 6 shows the four principal components that have eigenvalues greater than 1. The first principal component, shown in the column on the left, is indeed the one dealing with class inequality. It is interesting to note that the next three principal components are very close to those

TABLE 6: FACTOR ANALYSIS OF 9 MEASURES OF
PERCEIVED SERIOUSNESS OF GROUP INEQUALITY AND 4 MEASURES
OF CONCERN WITH CLASS INEQUALITY, CANADA, 1992

	I Class/ Income	II Quebec/ Francophones	III Minorities	IV English regions
Inequality experienced by ...				
Aboriginals/Natives	-.05	-.19	.81	.16
Women	.22	.38	.66	.07
Visible Minorities	.18	.20	.76	.01
Quebec	.20	.86	.07	.04
Ontario	.19	.56	-.10	.50
Atlantic Canada	.01	.33	.27	.63
The West	.12	.24	-.04	.76
Anglophones in Quebec	-.06	-.17	.13	.69
Francophones outside Quebec	.02	.77	.16	.11
Differences in income too large	.76	.06	.18	.12
Government responsibility to reduce income differences	.85	.05	.09	-.01
Government should provide jobs	.80	.20	-.02	-.08
Government should provide guaranteed basic income	.73	.05	.06	.09
Eigenvalue	3.71	1.99	1.52	1.18
% of total variance	28.5	15.3	11.7	9.1

previously reported in Table 1. That the first principal component of the enlarged matrix is the one dealing with class and income inequality means that the class and income variables explain more of the overall variance than any of the three sets of group inequality measures do. This suggests that opinions and beliefs about income inequality are more highly structured than are assessments of the seriousness of group inequalities. This information complements the related argument that class inequalities are indeed seen as more serious than the various types of group inequality, as suggested by Bennett's adjusted comparison of central tendencies.

Another important question concerns the nature of the linkage between these two types of inequalities. In a "zero sum model," the more awareness there is of one of these types, the less there is of the other. In this view, we literally would have *either* status/power group awareness *or* class awareness. To what extent is there evidence that, at the perceptual level, group (regional, language, and other) inequality masks, covers, impedes, or somehow takes away from, an awareness or appreciation of class or income inequality? This is a central theme of Canadian social science. Although the exact argument varies, the suggestion has been advanced in many forms that regional, linguistic, and, in the past, religious cleavages have had the effect, by virtue of their prominence, of in some sense overriding and obscuring class cleavages. In a "positive sum model," status/power group awareness reinforces class awareness, and/or vice versa. In this view, an awareness of group inequalities will lead to a greater awareness of class inequalities. This theme has appeared in different forms in many discussions about the link between class and language/ethnic/cultural cleavages in Quebec. (And at the empirical level, our results do show that Quebecers are more concerned about both group inequality and income inequality.)

If indeed it is the case that status/power group inequalities mask from view an awareness of class inequalities, then we would expect the correlation between measures of perceived group inequalities and perceived class inequalities to be negative. If, on the other hand, status group inequalities reinforce an awareness of class inequalities, we would expect the association to be positive. A third possible link would occur if the perceptions of the two types of inequalities were unrelated to each other, each set of perceptions responding to its own logic, as it were. It is possible to examine the nature of this linkage with the data at hand, and this is done in Table 7.

Table 7 presents the impact of the perceived seriousness of the nine group inequalities on a summary measure of concern about class inequality.[2] The multiple classification analysis format shows, for each independent variable, the raw and adjusted deviations from the grand mean of the dependent variable. Consider the first column of deviations that appears on the left-hand side of the table. These entries represent the bivariate relation between each independent variable on the left, dichotomized at the midpoint, and the dependent variable, the summary measure of concern for income inequality. The impact of perceived seriousness of women's inequality on concern about income inequality can be obtained as follows. Those respondents who see women's inequality as not at all serious or not very serious have a dependent variable score that is -.26 below the grand mean of 3.29; their score on the concern with income inequality variable is thus 3.03. Those respondents who see women's inequality as somewhat serious or very serious have a dependent variable score that is .12 above the grand mean; their score on the concern with income inequality variable is thus 3.41. The magnitude of this zero-order or bivariate relationship is given by the eta statistic, which here is equal to .18.

Turning to the right-hand column of Table 7, the corresponding entries are those that describe the effect of the independent variable *net of* the confounding effect of all the other independent variables. A measure of this net effect is given by the beta statistic, which here is equal to .09. A comparison of the left and right columns, and of eta and beta, tells us how much each zero-order relationship is modified when the other independent variables are taken into account simultaneously. Again, this particular panel of the table tells us that an awareness of women's inequality as serious is positively associated with a concern about income inequality, and that this relationship is weakened, but remains positive and statistically signficant, when the other independent variables are taken into account.

Several main findings are revealed by Table 7. First of all, it is evident that all but one of the nine types of perceived group inequality are positively associated with concern about income inequality. At the same time, most of these positive associations are modest, and only three of them remain statistically significant after controls. The strongest positive associations with concern about income inequality are the measures of perceived seriousness of Quebec inequality, of women inequality, and of visible minorities inequality.

The measure of inequality experienced by Anglophones in Quebec behaves in a distinct way. There is a different relation between the perceived inequality experienced by Anglophone Quebecers and the dependent variable. This is the only bivariate pair that shows a modest negative relationship, which is only strengthened after controls. This means that perceiving Anglophone Quebecers as suffering from serious inequality is negatively associated with a concern about income inequality. This exceptional pattern suggests that in some structural sense Anglophone Quebecers are being perceived as an economically privileged group, and that the inequality that this group suffers from is thus qualitatively different from that of the other groups on the list.

A region of residence variable is included among the independent variables, and the deviations on the left side illustrate the pattern already observed in the preceding section, namely that Quebec respondents are more concerned about income inequality than other Canadians. The association remains after controls, even if its magnitude is reduced. A comparison of the eta of .19 with the beta of .10 reveals that part, but only part, of Quebecers' greater concern with income inequality is explained by their different assessments of the seriousness of group inequality. The overall relationship can be summarized as follows.

TABLE 7: IMPACT OF PERCEIVED SERIOUSNESS OF 9 TYPES OF
GROUP INEQUALITY ON A SUMMARY MEASURE OF CONCERN
ABOUT INCOME INEQUALITY, 1992
(MULTIPLE CLASSIFICATION ANALYSIS)

Grand mean of dependent[1] variable = 3.29

Independent variable categories (N)	Unadjusted deviation	Eta	Adjusted deviation	Beta
Native/Aboriginal Inequality				
less serious (176)	-.06		-.08	
more serious (663)	.02		.02	
		.03		.04
Women Inequality				
less serious (261)	-.26		-.13	
more serious (578)	.12		.06	
		.18		.09**
Visible Minorities Inequality				
less serious (276)	-.21		-.12	
more serious (563)	.10		.06	
		.15		.09**
Quebec Inequality				
less serious (567)	-.18		-.12	
more serious (271)	.37		.25	
		.26		.18**
Ontario Inequality				
less serious (733)	-.05		-.02	
more serious (106)	.37		.11	
		.15		.04
Atlantic Inequality				
less serious (427)	-.08		.01	
more serious (412)	.08		-.01	
		.08		.01
The West Inequality				
less serious (628)	-.04		-.02	
more serious (211)	.12		.05	
		.07		.03
Anglophones in Quebec Inequality				
less serious (383)	.05		.07	
more serious (456)	-.04		-.05	
		.05		.06*
Francophones outside Quebec Inequality				
less serious (469)	-.14		-.01	
more serious (370)	.18		.01	
		.17		.01
Respondent's residence				
outside Quebec (635)	-.11		-.05	
inside Quebec (203)	.33		.16	
		.19		.10**

[1] The dependent variable, a summary measure of concern with income inequality, was constructed
by taking the mean value of each respondent's reply to the four measures shown in Table 5, with
1 = strongly disagree and 5 = strongly agree.
Multiple R = .329; Multiple R Squared = .109
* associated F statistic significant at .10 level; ** associated F statistic significant at .05 level

Quebecers are more concerned about income inequality than are other Canadians. They also tend to judge group inequalities to be more serious than other Canadians do, with some significant exceptions and a different pattern of concerns. These two types of perceptions are not reducible to each other, however, and Quebec respondents' greater concern with income inequality remains after the different pattern of perceptions of group inequalities is controlled for. Put differently, the results of Table 7 tell us that residence in Quebec, as well as concern for Quebec inequality, women inequality, and/or visible minority inequality, are all positively related to concern about income inequality. Especially interesting here is the fact that concern regarding aboriginal inequality, judged as a top priority in the English-majority provinces, is not associated with a concern for income inequality, whereas women inequality and visible minority inequality are so associated.[3]

◆

We have seen that the types of group inequalities ranked as most serious are somewhat different in Quebec than in the rest of Canada. What accounts for the different pattern of concerns in Quebec? It has already been suggested that Quebec respondents rank aboriginal inequality as less serious than do respondents in the rest of Canada because of the heightened tension between aboriginal nationalism and Quebec nationalism in the late 1980s and early 1990s, which came to a head with the defeat of the Meech Lake Accord in June of 1990, and with the events of the Oka crisis later that summer. This lower priority for Indian concerns in Quebec than elsewhere in Canada is consonant with the results of other surveys carried out since 1990. It also marks a reversal of the pattern repeatedly observed throughout the 1970s and early 1980s, in which Francophones and Quebecers were systematically *more* sympathetic toward Indian politics and aboriginal grievances than were Anglophones and residents of other provinces (see Laczko, 1995, chapter 8).

To some extent, the pattern of perceptions of group inequality observed in this survey may reflect the operation of what Horowitz (1991) has called an "economy of antipathies," whereby an increase in social distance between two groups in conflict is often accompanied by a corresponding decrease in social distance between each protagonist and some other group. In his study of South Africa, Horowitz found that after the events of Soweto in 1976 attitudes of Blacks and Afrikaans-speaking whites toward each other hardened, and at the same time mutual attitudes between Blacks and English-speaking whites became more positive. Using this logic, English Canadians may be favourably inclined to sympathize with aboriginal inequality partly as a disguised, or suddenly legitimate, way of ranking Quebec and Francophone concerns lower. In this connection, it might be mentioned that in the matrix of nine measures of group inequality, the bivariate correlation between native inequality and Quebec inequality is negative in the whole sample, but slightly positive in Quebec and in the rest of Canada if the two regional subsamples are examined separately. This means that the overall negative correlation is due to the fact that Quebecers assign a high priority to Quebec inequality and a lower priority to native inequality, and respondents elsewhere in Canada do the reverse.

Why has this displacement taken this particular form? No definitive answer to this question can be given here, but it is worth noting that the Quebec/Francophone versus English Canada/Anglophone polarization has modified the pattern of perceptions of aboriginal inequality, without modifying the pattern of assessments of women inequality and visible minorities inequality. The recent round of constitutional discussions and group polarization has not led to any major Quebec/Canada difference in assessments of women inequality, and the pattern whereby Quebec respondents rate this dimension as slightly more serious than those elsewhere is in keeping with the overall tendency of Quebecers to assign most of the dimensions a higher seriousness rating. Similarly, no significant difference in assessments of visible minorities inequality is evident between Quebec and the rest of Canada.

If the different pattern of concerns with respect to group inequalities can be understood as resulting from recent political dynamics, explanations for why Quebec respondents are more likely to assess group inequalities as serious in general, more likely to assess the degree of income inequality as large, and more likely to be in favour of state measures to reduce inequality, are still speculative. Of all the measures examined here, the only exceptions to the pattern of higher scores in Quebec than elsewhere are those dealing with aboriginals and with Anglophones in Quebec. On the whole, the tendency on the part of Quebec respondents to give higher assessments of both group and class inequality is consonant with the argument that minorities will often display greater awareness of all aspects of a power relationship.

. More research is needed on the determinants of these perceptions before the mechanisms behind the higher Quebec scores are fully understood. We might mention, however, that the differences observed in this chapter between respondents in Quebec and those in the rest of Canada are consonant with results from surveys on perceived French-English inequalities within Quebec. In recent decades, Francophones in Quebec have been systematically more likely than Anglophones to be aware of French-English inequalities and to judge them to be severe, and this tendency has been by and large maintained even as objective inequalities between the language communities have evened out. At the same time, Anglophones have developed some elements of a minority group outlook as well, and this shows up in the way they have come to perceive language inequalities in recent years (Laczko, 1995).

Further research is also needed to explore in detail the determinants of perceived income inequalities in various regions of Canada. What is behind Quebec's greater awareness of and concern about income inequality, and how does this correspond to objective conditions? Is Quebec's greater concern about income inequality related to the fact that there is more objective inequality in Quebec than in all but two other provinces (see Noel, 1993)? Is there a correlation between a province's or region's ranking in terms of its objective degree of inequality and its ranking in terms of perceived income inequality? Answers to these and similar questions will help chart the deeper dynamics behind the patterns reported in this paper.

Survey data are best seen as shaped and indeed created by the format used to gather them, and this data set is no exception. The format of the nine group inequality questions intentionally invited respondents to read their own meaning into the expression "suffer from inequality." Inequality can take many forms, and none was explicitly suggested in the questions as formulated. The special pattern of results obtained with respect to the Anglophones in Quebec category, for example, suggests that respondents resort to their own mix of class, status, and power criteria when faced with the group labels as stimuli, and that the mix is not identical for all of the labels. Our analysis reveals that Anglophones in Quebec appear to be simultaneously viewed in the rest of Canada as suffering from status or power inequality within Quebec, and at the same time as still enjoying a long-held position as a relatively affluent English-speaking region of Canada. This group is the object of much ambivalence, both within Quebec and elsewhere.

In this chapter we have examined, with one particular data set, the links between perceptions of two types of inequality in Canada. The results reported here have provided one particular glimpse of Canada's complex class, regional, linguistic, and ethnic stratification system in 1992. The ISSP data will allow this snapshot of the Canadian situation to be eventually put in a broader world perspective.

ENDNOTES

1. Another noteworthy difference between Quebec and the rest of Canada concerns attribution of responsibility for group inequality. The ISSP survey asked respondents whether responsibility lies with members of the group or with the rest of society. Quebec respondents were 8% more likely to attribute responsibility to the members of the group itself, and 10% less likely to attribute responsibility to the larger society. Given the number of cases, this difference is just statistically significant at the .05 level.

2. The measure of concern for income inequality is a constructed variable. It was created by taking the mean value, for each respondent, of replies to each of the four questions shown in Table 5.

3. This multiple classification analysis presents the results as if the independent variables combined additively in their impact on the dependent variable, and does not take any interaction effects into account. In fact, however, there are a few significant interraction effects present in the model, and a more detailed analysis would be required to fully chart the complexity of this multivariate relationship. More research is especially needed on the basic demographic and structural determinants of each set of perceptions, and on whether or not parallel or different factors are at work in Quebec and in the rest of Canada.

REFERENCES

Cairns, Alan C. (1986). The Embedded State: State-Society Relations in Canada, in Keith Banting (Ed.), *State and Society: Canada in Comparative Perspective* (53-86). Toronto: University of Toronto Press.

Goyder, John. (1990). *Essentials of Canadian Society.* Toronto: McClelland and Stewart.

Horowitz, Donald L. (1991). *A Democratic South Africa? Constitutional Engineering in a Divided Society.* Berkeley: University of California Press.

Laczko, Leslie S. (1994). Canada's Pluralism in Comparative Perspective. *Ethnic and Racial Studies, 17,* (1), 20-41.

Laczko, Leslie S. (1995). *Pluralism and Inequality in Quebec*. New York: St. Martin's Press and Toronto: University of Toronto Press.

Noel, Alain. (1993). Politics in a High Unemployment Society. In Alain-G. Gagnon (Ed.), *Quebec: State and Society* (2nd ed.) (422-49). Scarborough ON: Nelson Canada.

Pal, Leslie A. (1993). *Interests of State: The Politics of Language, Multiculturalism, and Feminism in Canada*. Montreal: McGill-Queen's University Press.

Pammett, Jon H. (1987). Class Voting and Class Consciousness in Canada. *Canadian Review of Sociology and Anthropology, 24*, (2), 269-90.

Ponting, J. Rick, & Roger Gibbins. (1980). *Out of Irrelevance: A Socio-Political Introduction to Indian Affairs in Canada*. Toronto: Butterworths.

CHAPTER SEVEN

GENDER AND INEQUALITY

Eileen Saunders

THE 1992 DATASET of the ISSP (International Social Survey Programme) permits the investigation of many aspects of gender differences in the perception of inequality.[1] The focus of the following discussion is on whether Canadian women see gender as playing a role in the structuring of inequality and to compare differences in perceptions between women and men and those within the category of women themselves. This provides the opportunity to address the issue of whether there exists a gendered *consciousness* of inequality, and, if it does exist, whether there is a gendered *discourse* about its causes or about policies in response to it. Among the issues to be addressed are opinions about the possible sources of social inequality (i.e., structural vs. individual), the legitimacy or illegitimacy of inequality, the proper role of the government in efforts to ameliorate inequality, and the degree of social conflict between particular groups.

GENDER, DIFFERENCE, AND GENDER GAPS

The documentation and explanation of structured inequality has long been a critical concern of feminist theory and research. As a result we have available to us several decades worth of studies of the national and international patterns of sex inequality, the mechanisms of its reproduction, and the extent of change over time in the major indicators of inequality. Less visible in the research has been a sustained focus on what women "think" about inequality, and whether their perceptions are different from those of men. Are there gender differences in the way women think about the causes of inequality? Do they recognize structured gender inequality as a problem? Are they more or less politically conservative than men in evaluating measures to reduce inequality? Such questions were relatively neglected in both the feminist and non-feminist literature on gender and inequality until the 1980s.

The reasons for the silence vary. In mainstream social science research, intellectual sexism certainly played its part in marginalizing these questions. When such questions were addressed, the analysis usually reflected questionable hypotheses and biased interpretations of the data.[2] Within feminist work as well, there was a certain reluctance to address the more general question of gender-based differences in attitudes and perceptions. As Rinehart notes, the feminist movement "had a great stake in denying differences when difference so often meant for women, relegation to an inferior position in sociopolitical terms" (1992, 9). Much of the preoccupation of liberal feminist theory and research throughout the 1970s was directed toward the erasure of difference, to demonstrate that women were equal to (i.e., "the same as") men in all capacities. The demonstration of differences between men and women was seen to provide the grounds upon which women were accorded different, and unequal, treatment. In such an intellectual climate it is not surprising that the "equality/difference" debates were particularly divisive within feminism.

In recent years there has been a renewed interest among both feminists and other researchers in the subject of gender-based differences. The shift in feminist discourse was reflected in both a revitalized interest in psychoanalytic explanations of sexual identity and in a reevaluation of "feminine qualities." Indeed, the rediscovery of gender differences has often been linked to a celebration of difference; the qualities and attitudes linked to women are seen as not only different from those of men but, indeed, superior. In the 1980s, as a result, "sexual difference came to be viewed as more intransigent, but also more positive, than most 1970s feminists had allowed" (Barrett & Phillips, 1992, 4). A related consequence of this valorization of difference was a renewed call by feminists for women to participate more fully and more actively in political life, "for their difference brings a necessary alternative perspective to the polis" (Rinehart, 1992, 10).

A more immediate and political source for the renewed interest in gender differences was the "discovery" by campaign strategists, media pundits, and academics alike of a significant gender gap in the voting patterns of men and women in the 1980 U.S. presidential election. Voting studies revealed an 8% gap between women and men in support for Republican Ronald Reagan, with men showing a stronger support for Reagan. This gender gap increased during the 1982 mid-term congressional elections, when 62% of men surveyed indicated support for Reagan's performance as President compared to 49% of women surveyed. Despite the landslide re-election of Reagan in 1984, a gender gap in voting was still apparent, with estimates ranging from a low of 6% to a high of 9% (Erie & Reim, 1988, 173; Klein, 1985, 33). These voting differences led to a flurry of "gender gap research" throughout the 1980s, most of it focused on voting patterns. These studies demonstrated the presence of this gap, in Canada and in other countries as well.[3]

The gender gap itself was not a new phenomenon, indeed there was evidence in the early days of survey research to suggest that men and women exhibited different interests and attitudes on a range of policy and political issues.[4] Political analysts, however, rarely saw these differences as large or particularly consequential. They took on a new significance in the 1980s, because they were seen to have affected the electoral process. As Jennings notes, sex differences in attitudes and perceptions "were viewed as less consequential, perhaps even as nuisances, by some, until a vital organ of the body politic was affected" (Mueller, 1988, 11). Party strategists and feminist activists alike considered the potential impact organized groups might have if they were able to mobilize a "women's vote." It led as well to more attention to sex differences in *policy preferences*, above and beyond voting differences, as political analysts attempted to chart the relation between sex and support for political issues. As Shapiro and Mahajan have argued, these gender-based differences "may take on a significance because of women's rising levels of political participation ... and because of the greater attention they may pay to particular issues and government policies" (1986, 44).

The gender gap research of this period was important for several reasons. As Rinehart notes, it helped to shift the analysis from "*women* and politics to *gender* politics," leading to a new value for comparative research on sex differences as well as for research on differences among *women* (1992, 13). This, in turn, led to a widening of our understanding of the idea of a gender gap beyond a simple concern with differences in voting choices to a broader focus on differences in political orientation, policy preferences, and political culture. The upshot was a flurry of empirical studies questioning conventional assumptions regarding women's political attitudes and preferences.

A long-held generalization, dating back to Maurice Duverger's 1955 text, *The Political Role of Women*, was that women were more conservative than men (Norris, 1988, 217). Surveys done in the 1980s on the relation between sex and voting choice and between sex and policy preferences began to challenge the validity of this assumption and, in fact, revealed evidence in support of the contradictory conclusion, that women were more liberal than men on a range of policy matters as well as in their voting preferences. Shapiro and Mahajan, for example, in their review of a series of U.S. opinion polls between 1972 and 1983, found that "Women's concerns are a mixture of economic liberalism, government activism, and traditional social conservatism (with some social liberalism as well)" (1986, 53). On the so-called "compassion issues," such as income redistribution, guaranteed jobs, and various welfare measures, women were consistently more liberal than men, and the differences between men and women were shown to have increased over the period of study. When it comes to questions regarding pornography, drugs, or crime, however, women are found to adopt more conservative views. Sue Tolleson Rinehart has argued that the socialization of women "prompts women toward *both* conserving and compassionate orientations ... because gender role socialization directs women toward the care and protection of others" (Rinehart, 1992, 158).

Kathryn Kopinak's analysis of Canadian data on gender differences in political attitudes demonstrates that not only do women show a higher support for social reform or charitable causes, they also "favour a redistribution of power in the workplace as well as a redistribution of valued goods and services by the government" (1987, 29). In a similar vein, McCormack summarizes the gender difference research as showing that "women, in all income groups, support measures that would provide greater economic security, more social services and a tax system that would redistribute wealth" (1991, 32). This support among women for more equalizing measures in society is reflected as well in their support for a more activist and interventionist government. As Klein notes in her analysis of these trends, when it comes to a range of domestic policy concerns, "women have tended to be more partial than men to government activism ... and more supportive than men of government efforts to help minorities and the poor" (1985, 35).

In her analysis of cross-national patterns in the gender gap, Pippa Norris found that while voting behaviour between European men and women in 1983 did not differ dramatically, there were significant gender differences on a range of issues, particularly in relation to the environment, the economy, and foreign policy. While there was no consistent pattern among the ten European countries she surveyed, "in all cases where there were significant sex differences, it was the women who were more left wing on the issues" (1988, 229). She further suggests that the appearance of this gender gap on policy issues may in fact increase significantly over time as differences are "currently suppressed in many European countries by the religiosity of older women" (1988, 223).

While the renewed interest in gender-based differences in political attitudes and preferences has been empirically fruitful, generating a variety of national and cross-national studies in recent years, it has been much less theoretically productive. It is one thing to document the existence of the gender gap in quantitative terms; it is quite another to account for its presence, shape, and distribution. In the aftermath of the 1980 and 1984 American presidential elections and the media attention given to the gender gap in voter behaviour, two very different interpretations were aired, one focusing on the argument that women are by nature different from men, possessing particular predispositions (for example, more caring and concerned for the unfortunate, or more family-focused in policy issues), and the other focusing on the argument that women share particular group interests and that the gender gap in Republican support was a consequence of women acting out of self-interests that differed from those of men.[5] In other words, if the policies of the Reagan administration were judged by women to undermine their interests, they would vote accordingly. Both interpretations are flawed. Adherents to the first find themselves endorsing a highly essentialist line of argument, wherein the sex/gender distinction is collapsed and intrasex differences are effectively ignored. Proponents of the women-as-interest-group position assume, without demonstrating, both a unity of interests among women, and a high degree of gender consciousness underlying women's political perceptions and preferences.

Other writers have since offered a number of alternative explanations for the existence of gender differences on a variety of social issues, with explanatory factors ranging from "maternal thinking" (Ruddick, 1980) to an "ethic of responsibility" that grounds a different morality for women (Gilligan, 1982) to the existence of a separate "political culture" inhabited by women, "which is more of a parallel and alternative culture rather than an oppositional or counter culture" (McCormack, 1991, 37). What underlies these various interpretations is a form of theoretical argument that Robert Connell calls "categoricalism." In such arguments, he notes, "the social order as a whole is pictured in terms of a few major categories—usually two—related to each other by power and conflict of interest" (1987, 54). The assumption of two "internally undifferentiated" and opposed categories, men and women, is problematic when trying to explain the gender gap in voting behaviour, because it fails to examine the role different women play in creating the gender gap.[6] The same is true of attitudes toward policy issues. Kopinak found, for example, that among *both* men and women there is "greater conservatism as one moves up the class and status hierarchies" (1987, 34).

Thus, while it is useful to examine where men and women differ in their perception of and attitudes toward particular issues, it is equally important to analyze where women differ from other women. We need to see attitude formation as a dynamic process that occurs in particular historical contexts; thus, the salience of certain issues for women has a historical dimension, and attitudes can change in response to changing social and economic circumstances.[7] Therefore, in response to the question, "does gender matter?," the prudent path is to consider under what conditions, or around what issues, gender might matter? One cannot take gender as a given identity that in all situations is the primary filter for the formation of attitudes; we need to examine which issues appear to mobilize a "gender consciousness" and which issues demonstrate similar gender support.

The notion of gender consciousness can serve as a starting point in examining women's understanding of social inequality, because it consists of "the recognition that one's relation to the political world is shaped in important ways by the physical fact of one's sex.... [It] may also carry a cognitive evaluation of the group's sociopolitical disadvantage, in absolute or relative terms, vis-à-vis other groups" (Rinehart, 1992, 14). As Patricia Gurin (1985) notes, there are many structural barriers in the way of developing a "gender consciousness," including an ideology of meritocracy that masks systemic inequality, the intertwining of the economic fates of men and women as members of the same family unit, class, or visible minority, and the sharing of the same cultural values among men and women through early childhood socialization. What we wish to ask is whether women in Canada demonstrate a gender consciousness: do they recognize women as economically and socially deprived relative to other groups in society? do they see gender as a factor in one's life chances? do they see the need for action to redress gender inequality?

A second task is to ask what interconnections Canadian women make regarding social inequality in general, its origins, and its legitimacy, and whether their attitudes differ from those of Canadian men. Where are women more likely to locate the causes and manifestations of inequality? under what circumstances do they see unequal treatment as legitimate? and what do they see as the responsibility of the state in measures to reduce inequality? These questions allow us to examine to what extent the "discourse of inequality" is a gendered discourse.

Finally, we need to ask what differences exist within the category of women in terms of gender consciousness and perceptions of inequality. What are the factors that interact with gender to influence their understanding of, and response to, inequality? Do variables, for example, such as nationality, age, education, and employment status significantly alter the shape of the gender gap? Here the international character of the ISSP data is particularly valuable because it allows us to probe the national variations in the character of the gendered discourse of inequality.

BELIEFS ABOUT GENDER INEQUALITY

There have been dramatic shifts in the social roles played by women over the last two to three decades, and significant improvements in their status in a number of areas, yet the available evidence points to a continuing marginalization of women in terms of their full participation in society. The 1994 edition of the *Women in the Labour Force* survey by Statistics Canada notes, among other findings, that while there has been tremendous growth in the participation of women in the labour force, there continues to be a heavy concentration of women in traditional "female" sectors, women earn significantly less than men, women are responsible for the majority of domestic labour in the home, and women are much more likely to be part-time workers (see also chapter 2 of this volume). By the late 1980s, many feminists were pointing to the growing problem of the "feminization of poverty," whereby the proportion of adults living in poverty who were female had increased significantly.[8] Though we know from empirical research that women have made significant gains in post-secondary education and now make up the majority of students in Canadian universities, their participation rate is still inversely related to the level of educational training; the higher one goes in postsecondary education the less likely one is to find women (Statistics Canada, 1994)[9] Finally, women continue to be significantly underrepresented in political institutions and processes. McCormack, for example, notes that in the 1988 Canadian federal election, "300 women ran for seats in the House, but only 39 were elected" (1991, 17).

In other words, when one examines the empirical evidence, the conclusion is clear: gender is a significant factor in the structure of inequality and the opportunities for mobility in our society, whatever the interpretation one may make for the underlying causes. It is therefore interesting to ask whether women share a recognition of gender as a factor in mobility and social inequality and to what degree this perception differs from men's recognition of gendered mobility and inequality? Three key questions in the ISSP survey allow us to examine beliefs about the role of gender in the structuring of opportunities and inequality.[10] The first question lists a series of thirteen factors, including gender, and asks respondents to indicate to what extent they believe each factor is important for "getting ahead in life" (see also chapter 4 of this volume). This allows us to analyze not only what males and females think about the importance of gender, but also how they rank its importance in relation to other factors. The second question of relevance asks for respondents' perceptions of group or regional inequalities in Canada. Again, we are able to explore to what extent women as a group are seen to suffer from inequality and how they are ranked relative to other groups or regions in Canada. In a third related question, respondents were asked to make a judgment regarding which groups or regions were more in need of action or intervention to change their situation. Accordingly, they were asked to choose the group or region that they think constitutes the "top priority for action."

In Table 1, it is immediately striking how close men and women are in their ranking of factors perceived to influence social mobility. Both men and women place greater emphasis on individual factors such as one's education, ability, ambition, or effort and relatively less emphasis on ascriptive characteristics such as sex, race, religion, or region of origin. It is, nevertheless, interesting that women and men have a different level of support for the importance of sex to social mobility; it figured as the ninth in importance for men and seventh for women. In terms of absolute support for sex as a factor in mobility, we see a 6% gender gap, with 11.3% of men and 17% of women identifying it as either essential or very

TABLE 1: RANK ORDER OF FACTORS IDENTIFIED AS ESSENTIAL OR
VERY IMPORTANT TO MOBILITY, BY SEX

	Males N=495	Females N=541
1	Good Education (84.6%)	Ambition (84.2%)
2	Ambition (84.4%)	Good Education (83.9%)
3	Hard Work (79.0%)	Hard Work (75.9%)
4	Natural Ability (45.2%)	Natural Ability (47.5%)
5	Know Right People (37.6%)	Know Right People (31.4%)
6	Well Educated Parents (29.1%)	Well Educated Parents (28.4%)
7	From Wealthy Family (16.7%)	Gender (17.0%)
8	Political Connections (14.2%)	Political Connections (11.1%)
9	Gender (11.3%)	From Wealthy Family (11.0%)
10	Race (10.9%)	Race (11.0%)
11	Region of Country (9.8%)	Region of Country (6.6%)
12	Political Beliefs (7.4%)	Political Beliefs (6.5%)
13	Religion (4.7%)	Religion (6.5%)

Note: Percentages refer to the respondents who indicated that a factor was either essential or very important for getting ahead in life.

important. One has to be careful of making too much of this gap, as it is evident that the large majority of *both* men and women do not see one's sex as being a particular advantage or disadvantage in getting ahead in life. In terms of a gender consciousness, as measured by the recognition of gender-related barriers to equality, then, women differ slightly from men in the importance they accord to sex, but do not display a high degree of gender consciousness. Their opportunities in life are not, for the most part, seen to be shaped by the opportunities of their "group"; rather, they are more likely, as with men, to see their opportunities as determined by individualistic factors. The top four factors identified as important by both men and women all resonate with an underlying ideology of meritocracy, in which individual competition and achievement are seen as more important than structural or group characteristics (see also chapter 4 of this volume).

When we look more closely at the level of absolute support among men and women for the role of sex in social mobility, we see more clearly the degree of similarity in beliefs. There are only slight differences between men and women in the absolute levels of support; while the strength of opinion on an item may very slightly, the overall direction of opinion does not. More significantly, one third of men *and* women believe that one's sex is not important at all to one's opportunities for social mobility in Canada.

TABLE 2: PERCEPTION OF HOW SERIOUSLY WOMEN SUFFER
FROM INEQUALITY, BY SEX

	(a) Males (%)	(b) Females (%)	Gender Gap (Diff. of a&b)
Very Serious	13.9	32.9	19.0%
Somewhat Serious	44.9	41.6	3.3%
Not Very Serious	28.0	19.2	8.8%
Not at All Serious	10.1	2.3	7.8%
No Response	2.9	4.1	1.2%

Note: Percentages in columns a and b do not total 100% because of rounding.

Yet when respondents are asked directly whether women as a group are treated equally in Canadian society, the data reveal a different story. As is shown in Table 2, over one-half of men and three-quarters of women believe that women in Canada suffer either very seriously or somewhat seriously from inequality. This apparent difference between perceptions about mobility and perceptions about inequality is interesting; men and women are more likely to affirm an ideology of equal opportunity for mobility when cued for the role of sex as an ascriptive variable. But when asked directly about how women as a group are treated, they are more likely to recognize the existence of structured inequality. It is significant, however, that men are much less likely to see this inequality as "very serious"; here the gap between men and women's response rate is almost 20%. Men are more likely to judge the unequal treatment of women as somewhat serious. Only 10% of the males and 2% of the females surveyed dismissed it altogether as a serious problem.

TABLE 3: GROUPS/REGIONS IDENTIFIED AS
SUFFERING FROM INEQUALITY
(VERY/SOMEWHAT SERIOUSLY), BY SEX

	(a) Males (%)	(b) Females (%)	Gender Gap (Diff. of a&b)
Natives/Aboriginals	74.9	75.6	0.7%
Women	58.8	74.5	15.7%
Visible Minorities	60.5	66.6	6.1%
Anglophones in Quebec	50.1	50.3	0.2%
Atlantic Canada	44.3	47.4	3.1%
Francophones outside Quebec	41.3	42.3	1.0%
Quebec	28.5	37.5	9.0%
The West	22.2	27.0	4.8%
Ontario	11.3	13.9	2.6%

TABLE 4: RANK ORDER OF GROUPS/REGIONS IDENTIFIED
AS DESERVING TOP PRIORITY FOR ACTION, BY SEX

	Males (%)	Females (%)
1	Natives/Aboriginals (46.8)	Natives/Aboriginals (31.9)
2	Women (14.4)	Women (31.6)
3	Quebec (12.1)	Visible Minorities (8.3)
4	Anglophones in Quebec (4.9)	Quebec (8.0)
5	Visible Minorities (4.7)	Anglophones in Quebec (3.4)
6	Atlantic Region (4.1)	Atlantic Region (3.4)
7	Francophones Outside Quebec (2.8)	Ontario (1.6)
8	The West (2.3)	Francophones Outside Quebec (1.2)
9	Ontario (0.4)	The West (1.0)

Note: The above percentages do not total 100% because the table does not include answers that identified "no inequality" (which was approximately 4% for both males and females), or those that gave no response.

Tables 3 and 4 give the larger context to male and female perceptions about group or regional inequality. Respondents were asked to judge the severity of inequality suffered by nine different groups or regions of Canada, including women as one identified group, and then were asked to pick the group or region that most deserved immediate priority for intervention to alter its situation. As we see in Table 3, the gap between the perceptions of men and women regarding the extent of inequality for various groups and regions is very slight, except in regard to their beliefs about the inequality of women. The average of the other gaps combined is 3.8%; the gender gap regarding perceptions about women's inequality is 15%. The other gap of interest, while not as large, is noteworthy. Women were somewhat more inclined to see Quebec as suffering from very serious or somewhat serious inequality than men were. There appears to be a consensus among men and women regarding which groups are perceived to suffer from inequality and to what degree, with the notable exception of women's inequality. And here, the difference between men and women is more in the strength rather than the direction of their support for a particular opinion. Their views on some groups are strikingly close; for example with respect to native groups or Anglophones living in Quebec, the gap between their levels of support is less than 1%. It is further interesting that for every group or region listed, women show a higher level of absolute support than men for the perception of inequality, even though the difference is quite small in several cases.

Table 4 summarizes respondents' views regarding the group or region most in need of action to redress its situation. Slightly over 60% of male and female respondents chose either aboriginal groups or women as the group most in need of action, but the different levels of support for each is noteworthy. Almost equal numbers of female respondents saw native groups or women as the top priority, while close to half of the males identified native groups as the most in need of action, with women being chosen by only 14% (with Quebec running a very close third with 12% of male support). There is little support for any of the other identified groups or regions; for example, while 60% of males claimed that visible minorities suffer from serious inequality in Canada (see Table 3), only slightly over 4% see them as deserving top priority in action.

What do these patterns tell us regarding beliefs about gender inequality? First, that there are more similarities than differences in opinions between men and women. Their perceptions about mobility and opportunity reflect a high degree of similarity, both on relative ranking and level of support, regarding the factors that influence one's life chances. Despite an array of empirical evidence that demonstrates that women are objectively deprived relative to men on many social indicators, the large majority of both men and women do not see gender as playing an important role in shaping opportunities. Indeed, the three top factors for both men and women are all factors where individual achievement figures prominently: getting a good education, having high ambitions, and working hard. Second, the majority of men and women do believe that women as a group suffer from inequality, although female respondents are more likely to label it as very serious inequality than are male respondents. When we look at this pattern in conjunction with the first, it appears that a recognition of group inequality can easily coexist with the assumption of an equal and meritocratic opportunity structure. Women may be unequal, but the fact that they are women is not perceived to have made them unequal!

Finally, men and women are very similar in how they rank the degree of inequality of different groups and the relative priority of need for change, but men show less absolute support for women as an unequal group on both of these dimensions. The latter is interesting in the light of some previous research that has demonstrated that men show more support than women for gender equality, and for redressing the disparities of gender.[11] In our sample, almost a third of the women agree with men that aboriginal groups are in need of top priority, but an equal proportion of women say gender inequality should be tackled first. All other groups fall considerably behind in priority for action.

GENDERED BELIEFS ABOUT SOCIAL INEQUALITY?

Aside from how men and women think about the role of gender in inequality, we are interested as well in the more general question of how they think about inequality itself, its causes, manifestations, and justifications. Is inequality seen to flow from structural factors or, rather, is it attributed to personal failing? Is there evidence to suggest a more "compassionate orientation" among women in the way they think about inequality and, related to this, do women adopt a more proactive stance in terms of government intervention? Under what circumstances do women justify economic disparities, and does this differ from men? Where do they see the major divisions in terms of social conflict in Canada today? An exploration of the ISSP data relating to these questions allows us to consider whether the discourse about inequality in Canada is, indeed, a gendered discourse, and, if so, to what extent.

TABLE 5: PERCEPTION OF RESPONSIBILITY FOR
GROUP INEQUALITY, BY SEX

	(a) Males (%)	(b) Females (%)	Gender Gap (Diff. of a&b)
Individual	23.1	15.1	8%
Society	69.0	74.3	5.3%
No Inequality	4.0	5.5	1.5%
Don't Know	4.0	5.1	1.1%

Note: Percentages in column (a) do not total 100% because of rounding.

One might expect that, given the emphasis on achievement factors in beliefs about social mobility addressed in Table 1, both men and women would tend to emphasize individual factors as the primary cause of inequality. This is not the case. When respondents were explicitly asked to judge whether a group or region's inequality was due to social or personal causes, the large majority of both sexes chose social causes. This is quickly evident in Table 5; 69% of males and 74% of women priorize social causes of inequality. The largest gap between men and women (at 8%) is in relation to support for individual explanations of inequality. Almost one quarter of men see inequality as something that a group or region brings on itself through its own actions, a somewhat higher level of support than women express.

As a further probe of opinions regarding the origins and persistence of inequality, respondents were asked to agree or disagree with a series of seven statements, each offering a different potential reason for inequality (see chapter 4 of this volume). Underlying three of the statements is the notion of inequality as a result of individual effort and ability; two statements emphasize a more critical argument in which the role of class figures more prominently (i.e., that inequality continues because it benefits the rich or because ordinary citizens are too apathetic to eliminate it). The remaining two statements suggest the necessity of inequality for national prosperity and the benefit of all. As Smith notes, in an earlier ISSP study using similar statements, they can be seen as three different types of explanation for inequality: incentives, class conflict, and general economic prosperity (1989, 69-70). In his comparison of the relative popularity of the three explanations across seven countries, he found that incentives and class conflict were the most popular explanations, and the promotion of economic prosperity was the least popular. A similar pattern is evident here in the responses of Canadian men and women.

TABLE 6: RANK ORDER OF SUPPORT FOR EXPLANATIONS OF
INEQUALITY AND INCOME DISPARITIES, BY SEX

	Males	Females
1	Incentive for Long Years of Study (61.9%)	Inequality Benefits the Rich (65.2%)
2	Incentive for Extra Responsibility (59.3%)	Incentive for Long Years of Study (63.4%)
3	Inequality Benefits the Rich (59.1%)	Incentive for Extra Responsibility (61%)
4	Incentive for Skills and Qualifications (46.0%)	Incentive for Skills and Qualifications (54.1%)
5	Inequality Due to Apathy (44.0%)	Inequality Due to Apathy (46.3%)
6	Business Profits Benefit All (40.4%)	Business Profits Benefit All (37.2%)
7	Large Income Differential Good for Prosperity (17.8%)	Large Income Differential Good for Prosperity (15.0%)

Note: The percentages in brackets refer to the percentage of males and of females who either agreed or strongly agreed with the statement.

Table 6 describes the relative support, in rank order, of men and women for the different explanations of the persistence of inequality and economic disparities. Again, we find more similarity than difference in their responses. Both men and women show very little support for arguments that justify inequality on the basis of general prosperity, and are more likely to agree that income disparities are necessary to motivate people to undertake extra responsibility or to invest time and effort in extra training and years of professional study. Nevertheless, the explanation that was the most popular among women, with 65% of female support, was that which linked inequality to class power and privilege. The majority of men also agreed with this explanation; but with 59% support among male respondents, it ranked third in popularity behind financial incentives for taking on extra responsibility and for rewarding long years of professional education. Men and women are roughly similar in their support for the idea that the apathy of "ordinary people" prevents the elimination of inequality. The largest gap in opinion between men and women is 8%, and is more a matter of strength of support than direction: 54% of women and 46% of men think pay differentials are necessary to motivate workers to acquire skills and qualifications.

Another way to uncover gender differences in attitudes about inequality is to consider under what circumstances individuals see income disparities as justified. Respondents were therefore asked to judge how important different factors *should* be in determining income, or, in other words, what underlying conditions could justify income differences? Men and women have a comparable assessment of what factors should be central to the income one receives; the large majority of both agree that how well one performs a job, how much responsibility one has on the job, and how hard one works are the top three factors that *should* matter. Not only is the order in which they identified factors as important almost identical, there are only slight differences in the level of support for each factor. Men and women both appear to place a high premium on individualistic factors of achievement and performance and less emphasis on the economic demands of family and children. Half of the women sampled said that what is needed to support a family should be either essential or very important in determining an individual's income; slightly less than half of the males agreed. Receiving the lowest level of support as a factor that should be important to income determination was the consideration of whether a person has children to support; 42% of females and 36% of males saw it as a central factor, a gap of 6%. For both sexes, then, the individual contributions one makes to his or her job, or the personal qualities one brings to it, outweigh the domestic and familial responsibilities one bears in deciding appropriate reward structures. If "maternal thinking" is thought to be a predisposition that underlies women's attitudes on a range of political concerns, it does not explain why we find a lesser emphasis given to family and children. On this issue women and men are very much in agreement: income levels and income disparities should be first tied to individual performance, responsibility, and effort.

Related to the above issue is the question of whether current income disparities in Canada are perceived to be acceptable or not, and the perceived role of government in the reduction of disparities (see chapter 4). When men and women were asked directly whether they thought income differences are too large in Canada, the majority of both agreed. Women, however, were more likely to think the disparities were too large: 76.4% of Canadian women sampled and 61.3% of the men either agreed or strongly agreed that income differences are too large, a gender gap of 15%. Only 17.2% of men and 8.4% of women thought the disparities were acceptable.[12] They were then asked to agree or disagree with statements about whether it was the responsibility of government to reduce

TABLE 7: PERCEPTION OF GOVERNMENT RESPONSIBILITY FOR
REDUCING INEQUALITY, BY SEX

	(a) Males (%)	(b) Females (%)	Gender Gap (Diff. of a&b)
Should Reduce Income Difference:			
AGREE	39.6	51.8	12.2%
DISAGREE	37.3	23.0	14.3%
Should Provide Jobs For All:			
AGREE	35.2	44.2	9.0%
DISAGREE	43.5	34.0	9.5%
Should Guarantee Basic Income			
AGREE	40.5	54.1	13.6%
DISAGREE	42.0	32.3	9.7%

Note: The percentages in columns a and b do not total 100%, because they do not include the response categories "neither agree nor disagree" and "can't choose."

these disparities, and whether the government should provide guaranteed basic incomes and guaranteed jobs for all.

In Table 7, we see that on all three issues (reducing income disparities, providing jobs for all who want them, and ensuring a guaranteed basic income to all), women show a higher level of support, with the gender gap ranging between 9% and 14%. Over half of the women agreed that government should reduce income disparities between those with high and low incomes, and should provide a guaranteed basic income; slightly less than half also believe government should provide jobs to all. In each case, however, more women agree with these perceived responsibilities than disagree. As for men, on two of the possible modes of government intervention, providing jobs and guaranteeing a basic income, they are more likely to disagree than agree. These results would suggest that women, to a greater degree than men, support government intervention on the so-called "compassion issues" of income redistribution, job provision, and guaranteed income, a finding consistent with research discussed earlier in this chapter.

When it comes to using the taxation system as a mechanism for the redistribution of income, gender differences all but disappear. On the ISSP survey, respondents were asked whether they thought people with high incomes should pay a different share of their income in taxes compared to low income people. Approximately 72% of men and 74% of women think high income people should pay either a larger or a much larger share of their income in taxes; slightly over 20% of each thought they should pay the same share as low income people. There is, in other words, a strong consensus among men and women that the operation of the taxation system should take into account income inequalities.

Do men and women think differently about social conflict between different groups in society? Their perceptions on social conflict can provide a clue to what individuals think are the major social divisions underlying inequality. The ISSP survey asked respondents to judge the severity of conflict between six different pairs of social groups: poor people and rich people, the working class and the middle class, the unemployed and people with jobs, management and workers, farmers and city people, and young people and older people. (It is unfortunate, for our purposes, that men and women were not identified as one of the pairs.) We can see in Table 8 that men and women share very similar views on where major conflict does or does not exist in Canada. In most cases, the majority of men and women do not report strong levels of social conflict between these groups, with the conflict between the working class and the middle class being perceived as the least severe. One exception is the grouping of management and workers, which exhibits, according to the majority of both men and women, strong or very strong conflict. There are notable gaps in the level of support between men and women for the severity of conflict between rich and poor people and employed and unemployed people. Women are more apt to judge the conflict within these two groupings as strong or very strong; the gender gap ranges between 11% and 12%. Of the six paired groupings listed, rich/poor and employed/unemployed are the ones most evidently marked by inequality. Women are, in other words, more likely to show a higher degree of concern for the level of conflict between those groups most clearly identified as the "haves" and the "have-nots." It is also interesting to note that men were more likely than women to indicate that they saw no conflict at all between these groups. Even though the absolute numbers were low (ranging from 2% to 27% of male respondents) for each of the six groupings, with the sole exception of management and workers, men were more likely than women to indicate that there was no conflict between the groups.

TABLE 8: PERCEPTION OF VERY STRONG/STRONG CONFLICT
BETWEEN SOCIAL GROUPS, BY SEX

	(a) Males (%)	(b) Females (%)	Gender Gap (Diff. of a&b)
Management and Workers	57.5	57.7	0.2%
Rich and Poor	36.8	48.1	11.3%
Unemployed and People with Jobs	26.8	39.6	12.8%
Young and Old	22.6	27.4	4.8%
Farmers and City People	17.8	23.7	5.9%
Working And Middle Class	12.8	14.0	1.2%

In reviewing the findings discussed in this section, then, is there a basis to talk about social inequality as a gendered discourse? Do we see that men and women think differently about social inequality? The answer, as before, is both yes and no. When it comes to attributing cause to structural or individual factors the gap between men and women is slim, and the strong majority of both genders agree that the origins of inequality lie with society and not the individual. They both display scepticism regarding functionalist explanations of inequality that stress the socio-economic benefits of income disparities, i.e., that large business profits or income differences can be justified on the basis of the "social good." The majority of men and women, in comparable numbers, explain inequality both as being linked to a need for financial incentives to motivate individuals and as being a result of the vested interests of affluent groups. A similar consensus was found regarding perceptions of justifiable income differences. A strong meritocratic ideology is apparent in the responses of both men and women when it comes to rationalizing income disparities. Both are more willing to accept disparities that can be justified on the basis of individual performance, responsibility and effort, and less willing to accept economic need (in terms of family subsistence) as a basis for income calculations. Finally, we see that men and women tend to agree on the major divisions underlying social conflict, although women are somewhat more likely than men to see the conflict between the rich and the poor and between the employed and the unemployed as severe.

Where we can begin to see gender play a role in perceptions about inequality is in relation to the question of intervention and social change. Women exhibit a stronger preference for government action to reduce inequality and to guarantee a minimum level of economic security. While both agree that income differences are too large in Canada, men are less supportive than women of the responsibility of government to redress this situation. Whether this is an indication of a more compassionate orientation among women for the economically disadvantaged, or whether it is a reflection of self-interest on the part of women as a more economically marginal group, cannot be determined from this survey data. We do know, however, that this difference is consistent with the findings of other research on the more liberal leanings of women on social policy issues.

The discourse of inequality, then, appears to become a gendered discourse, not in relation to the causes, manifestations, or justifications of inequality; here an underlying ideology of meritocracy appears to inform the perceptions of both men and women. Rather, the discourse of inequality takes on a gendered character in regard to the modification or transformation of inequality. Both sexes recognize social inequality as a problem, but women adopt a more proactive stance on the perceived responsibility of government to reduce inequality.

WOMEN'S PERCEPTIONS OF GENDER INEQUALITY

In this final section of our examination of the role of gender in perceptions of inequality, we turn to the question of difference *within* the category of women. The resurgence in interest in the question of difference in 1980s feminist thought, as discussed earlier, was not restricted to differences between men and women. Within feminist analyses, debate centred around the essentialist assumptions attached to the concept of "woman," precipitating a rejection by many feminists of the notion of woman as a universal category. "Woman" is a social construct, it was argued, and as such it is mediated by a set of other differentiations, such as class, race, age, education, etc. Consequently, in order to examine the gendered nature of perceptions of inequality we must take account of intrasex differences in perception. It is not our intention here to engage in a detailed examination of the interaction of each possible demographic variable with gender in forming the full range of perceptions about inequality. Rather, we are most interested in the question of whether women in Canada exhibit a "universal" consciousness of gender and its role in inequality, or whether the salience of this issue varies across demographic groupings of women. We therefore examine a few key demographic variables in order to test whether and to what degree women demonstrate a consensus in the way they think about the role of gender in inequality.

The key demographic variables we will examine are nationality, age, education, personal income, employment, marital status, and language. The choice of these variables, while not exhaustive, allows us to consider a range of factors related to class, domestic situation, and cultural context. The obvious demographic variable missing here is race. On the ISSP survey, respondents were asked "To which ethnic or cultural groups did your *ancestors* belong?"—a question that cannot be used nonproblematically to determine the respondent's race for purposes of correlation. While an examination of the interaction of race and gender in the formation of attitudes would be valuable, particularly in a discussion of inequality, it was felt that the ambiguous nature of the question for our purposes precluded its investigation.

We turn first to the question of cross-national patterns in women's perception of the role of gender in social mobility. As noted in the beginning of this chapter, our focus is on the examination of gender and inequality in the Canadian context. The international character of the ISSP data, however, also provides a valuable opportunity to explore the role of national culture in attitude formation, something that is taken up in more detail in other chapters in this collection. For our purposes, it is useful to ask to what degree Canadian women assess the role of gender in inequality in a manner similar to women in other countries. As noted in earlier discussion, women in the Canadian sample of this survey essentially agreed with men that gender was not very significant in determining one's life chances, although they also felt that women as a group suffered from serious inequality. Because the question regarding group inequality was only included on the Canadian version of the survey, we cannot explore the cross-national comparisons on this issue. Nevertheless, we can examine to what extent women in different countries believe that one's gender is a factor in social mobility.

TABLE 9: RANK ORDER OF COUNTRIES (FEMALES ONLY)
PERCEIVING ONE'S GENDER AS ESSENTIAL OR VERY IMPORTANT
TO MOBILITY

	COUNTRY	%
1	Philippines	59.2
2	Russia	25.7
3	United States	19.2
4	Austria	19.0
5	Poland	19.0
6	Germany (East)*	17.4
7	Canada	16.6
8	Germany (West)*	16.4
9	Italy	16.1
10	Bulgaria	15.1
11	Sweden	15.0
12	New Zealand	14.1
13	Great Britain	13.6
14	Slovenia	12.8
15	Czech Republic	10.4
16	Norway	8.6
17	Hungary	7.9

Note: The percentages in the third column include responses that identified one's sex as either essential or very important to social mobility.
* For analytic purposes the German data are separated to reflect those regions of the country that were *formerly* East and West Germany.

In Table 9, we can see the rank ordering of countries in terms of women's perceptions of gender as an "essential" or "very important" factor in social mobility. With a few notable exceptions, it is evident that there is not a great difference between the women respondents in the various countries regarding the importance they attach to gender. In only one country, the Philippines, is gender rated as essential or very important by a majority of the women; the large majority of women in all the other countries do not attach much significance to its role in one's opportunities in life, and the gap between the countries seldom reaches more than 7%. In Norway and Hungary, less than 10% of the women surveyed saw it as a key factor. In terms of a cross-national pattern, then, national culture does not seem to alter significantly women's perceptions of social mobility as an "ungendered" phenomenon. It is important to note, however, that one cannot infer from this that female respondents in these countries would perceive that women as a group are treated equally to men. As noted earlier with regard to the Canadian sample, when one is asked directly about group inequality, as opposed to factors in individual opportunities and mobility, the perception can change significantly.

In turning to the impact of other demographic variables on women's perceptions within the Canadian sample, we felt it important to examine differences in their understanding of the significance of gender to mobility and of the extent and urgency of female inequality. From the earlier discussion of the data, we know that the large majority of women respondents had chosen four factors as the most important to social mobility: having a good education, being ambitious, working hard, and having a natural ability; in fact, one third of women believed that gender has no role in social mobility. Nevertheless, women were inclined to agree that women suffer from inequality and that they deserve top priority among other groups for action to redress this inequality. Therefore, for each of the remaining demographic variables we examined perceptions of the importance of gender to mobility as well as perceptions regarding the extent and urgency of female inequality.

TABLE 10: WOMEN'S PERCEPTIONS OF MOBILITY AND FEMALE INEQUALITY, BY AGE, IN PERCENTAGES

	18-24 N=80	25-34 N=120	35-44 N=96	45-54 N=67	55-64 N=58	65+ N=75
Women Suffer from Very Serious Inequality	36.1	30.2	35.6	45.8	33.3	23.9
Women Deserve Top Priority in Action	34.3	34.4	37.9	41.0	21.9	18.3
Gender Is Essential or Very Important to Mobility	13.2	16.5	15.9	25.9	23.9	11.9

In Table 10, the impact of age is examined, and we can begin to see the appearance of variations in perception. The highest level of support for the significance of gender to mobility is found among women between the ages of 45 and 64, where roughly one-quarter perceive it as a central factor. The lowest level is among women over the age of 65 and under 25, where only a little more than 10% perceive gender as significant to mobility. If we consider that women aged 45 to 64 would more likely include the first generation of women who grew up under the influence of the women's movement, as well as that generation of women that experienced dramatic increases in labour force participation throughout the '60s and

'70s, it is perhaps not at all surprising that this age cohort is more likely to perceive the significance of gender in life's opportunities. The majority of all age groups agreed that education, ambition, and hard work were the most significant factors in mobility, with natural ability coming a close fourth, although with varying levels of support. More women over 65, for example, were likely to explain mobility on the basis of natural ability yet attached less significance than other age groups to the importance of a good education. The youngest group of women attached the highest level of support to a good education, not surprising if we consider that this cohort is more likely to be engaged in postsecondary education or just entering the labour market with degree in hand. Still, the underlying pattern for all age groups is an understanding of mobility as linked to meritocratic processes and not as the result of ascriptive characteristics.

The impact of age on women's perceptions of inequality and gender can also be seen in their responses to the questions concerning the severity of inequality experienced by women in Canada and the priority they should receive, relative to other groups or regions, in action designed to bring about social change. As we can see in Table 10, women of different age groups are quite similar in the extent to which they see women as suffering from "very serious" inequality, with the exception of women ages 44 to 54 and women over the age of 65. The former are more likely to see women as suffering very serious inequality; almost half of the women in this age group reflected this belief. Their stronger perception of women's inequality is also reflected in the priority they give to intervention on behalf of women; they are twice as likely than women older than them to claim that women deserve top priority over other groups. In comparison, natives, who were ranked second in priority, received only a 25% level of support among those in this age category.

For women aged 65 and older, on the other hand, less than one quarter believe that women suffer from very serious inequality and they show little support for women receiving priority in intervention (indeed, 50% of this group felt that aboriginal groups deserved top priority). In the age groups between 18 and 44, there is not a great deal of difference in how they perceive either the severity of inequality faced by women, or how urgently it should be redressed. In other words, the differences in perception appear stronger among the older groups of women, where we find what could be termed a division between more feminist views and more traditional views on the subject of women's inequality. Age itself does not have an independent impact on women's perceptions of female inequality;

we need to consider the historical context in which different generations of women came of age. For those women born before World War II, the vestiges of a more traditional understanding of women's proper role are still apparent. For women who came of age in the '50s and who were the first wave of women to enter the labour force in large numbers on a permanent basis, there is more recognition of the injustices suffered by women and of the need to change this situation. This difference can also be partially attributed to the effects of the women's movement; throughout the 1960s and '70s, this age cohort of women was the first to be exposed to the consciousness-raising efforts of organized feminism. While this does not imply that younger age cohorts have lapsed into a new conservatism regarding women's issues, it does suggest that the *salience* of the women's inequality as an issue is not as strong among women in their twenties and early thirties.

TABLE 11: WOMEN'S PERCEPTIONS OF MOBILITY AND FEMALE INEQUALITY, BY EDUCATION, IN PERCENTAGES

	Grade School or Some High School N=80	Finished High School N=144	Some College or University N=113	Finished College or University N=153	Graduate School N=49
Women Suffer Very Serious Inequality	41.3	24.6	25.7	34.0	57.3
Women Deserve Top Priority in Action	23.7	30.4	29.8	31.4	51.3
Gender is Essential or Very Import to Mobility	17.5	10.4	13.0	20.1	40.5

When we turn to the question of the impact of educational differences among women, we see the liberalizing influence of higher levels of education on women's perceptions regarding the importance of gender to social mobility. In Table 11, women with graduate school education were three times as likely to see gender as a central factor in one's life chances compared to women with a high school education, and even twice as likely as women with a university or college degree. This is consistent with other research, which has demonstrated the relation of increased educational opportunities to increased dissatisfaction with traditional roles for women and increased sympathy for feminist views. Klein (1985), Gurin (1985), and Rinehart (1992) have all demonstrated the correlation of increased education with a higher level of "gender consciousness," i.e., a stronger degree of identification with women as a group. Partially we can attribute this effect to the intellectual environment encountered by women in university education, an environment in which women encounter nontraditional views; yet we cannot ignore the connection between class origins and educational access.

When we considered women's support for other factors as central to mobility, we found that women of different educational levels show varying support for the centrality of a good education, the largest gap being between women with a graduate school education and those with either grade school or some high school. Although we find a direct relation here between level of education and the importance accorded to a good education in life, it is also important to remember that a large majority of all groupings saw a good education as very significant. Women with the lowest levels of education, grade school and some high school, were those least likely to see it as a central factor; their strongest factor support was for ambition. They also showed less support than other women for hard work and natural ability as factors central to mobility,[13] while women with the highest educational levels were the least likely to choose personal ambition as an essential or very important factor.

In Table 11, we also examined the impact of educational level on perceptions of the degree of women's inequality and the urgency for change. The women most likely to say that females as a group suffer from "very serious inequality" lie at opposite ends of the educational spectrum; 41.3% of the grade school/some high school group and 57.3% of the graduate school group share this perception. The difference is that women with graduate school education are more likely to see women's inequality as needing immediate action, with over half of the women in this cohort sharing this view; women with grade school or some high school education, on the other hand, are the least likely to see a need to intervene on behalf of women. There is certainly a more activist orientation regarding gender to be found among highly educated women, and, not surprisingly, they display the highest degree of gender consciousness of all educational cohorts in the survey. There are not large gaps between the other cohorts when it comes to recognizing women as deserving priority in social change initiatives; in all cases less than a third of the women share this view and show, instead, stronger support for native groups as those most deserving.

TABLE 12: WOMEN'S PERCEPTIONS OF MOBILITY AND FEMALE
INEQUALITY, BY PERSONAL INCOME, IN PERCENTAGES

	Under $15,000 N=171	$15,000-$24,999 N=98	$25,000-$34,999 N=100	$35,000-$44,999 N=64	$45,000+ N=39
Women Suffer Very Serious Inequality	32.3	28.7	35.9	34.9	46.2
Women Deserve Top Priority in Action	31.3	30.6	31.0	20.6	38.5
Gender Is Essential or Very Import. to Mobility	13.8	14.6	12.8	37.0	23.1

In the examination of the impact of income on women's attitudes toward gender, mobility, and inequality, personal income was chosen over household income because it has been found in the past to be a better discriminator for women when measuring gender identification (see, for example, Rinehart, 1992, 55-56). In Table 12, we can see that there are significant gaps in women's perceptions of the importance of gender to mobility. Again, as with educational level, we find that the higher income groups of women are more likely to see gender as a central factor than lower income groups; still, the majority of all women perceive it as not very important. The stronger perception of the importance of gender among higher income women is perhaps logical; as women get better jobs and earn larger incomes, they are likely to become more sensitized to the role of gender when competing with men in the labour force. Women who are in lower income positions are more likely to be found in the female ghettos of labour (such as service occupations and clerical positions), where they are less likely to compete on the basis of gender.

The presence of a stronger consciousness of gender and its role in inequality among high income women is also borne out in responses to the other two questions that address female inequality. As we see in Table 12, almost half of the women earning over $45,000 per year felt that female inequality was very serious; the other income groups do not vary greatly on this question, with levels of support ranging between 28 and 35%. The gap in perceptions between the income groups is smaller on the question of priority for intervention, except for women earning between $35,000 and $45,000, who demonstrated a lower level of support (at 20.6%) than the other income groups for the priority of women. In any case, income level does not appear to be as significant a discriminator of attitudes concerning intervention in women's inequality as it is for attitudes concerning the severity of women's inequality.

The impact of employment status on perceptions of gendered inequality was also addressed, specifically in terms of whether perceptions shifted between those employed full-time (i.e., more than 35 hours per week) and those employed on a part-time basis (i.e., less than 35 hours per week). The expectation was that women more fully engaged in the labour force would be in a position to experience more directly the consequences of their gender for mobility (i.e., in terms of disparities in pay scales, promotion opportunities, workplace culture, etc.) than women who had a less permanent attachment to the labour force. In Table 13, we see that full-time employees *are* more likely to attach importance to the role of gender in social mobility; there is a 15% gap between their level of support for gender as a central factor and that of part-time employees. There were no significant gaps in the perceptions of each group regarding the relative importance of the four leading factors of education, ambition, hard work, and ability. Both in rank and level of support for these factors, both groups of women are very close in their perceptions; it is only in the weight they give to gender that we see a larger gap appear. This difference is also reflected in beliefs about female inequality as shown in Table 13. Women who are employed full-time show a somewhat stronger level of support for the belief that female inequality is a very serious problem; well over a third of these respondents supported this belief. The difference in level of support between the two groups on this question is 10%. Yet, we do not see this difference carried over into their perceptions regarding the urgency or priority of need for female inequality to be addressed in social action; in fact, here part-time employees show a somewhat higher level of support (with a difference of 7%). It is therefore difficult to conclude that employment status is a strong predictor of women's attitudes toward gender inequality; at best, we can say there is some evidence to suggest that women who are employed full-time are more conscious of gender as important to one's opportunities, and are somewhat more likely to consider female inequality to be a very serious problem. This heightened degree of gender consciousness, however, does not necessarily make them more activist regarding social change.

TABLE 13: WOMEN'S PERCEPTIONS OF MOBILITY AND FEMALE
INEQUALITY, BY EMPLOYMENT STATUS, IN PERCENTAGES

	Employed Full-time N=221	Employed Part-time (a) N=103
Women Suffer Very Serious Inequality	37.8	27.2
Women Deserve Top Priority in Action	29.4	36.9
Gender Is Essential or Very Important to Mobility	23.4	7.8

Note: (a) includes those respondents employed 15 to 35 hours weekly and those employed less than 15 hours or temporarily out of work.

The importance of marital status as a demographic variable has yielded different results in the research to date, with its predictive value dependent on the nature of the issue being examined. There is evidence to suggest, for example, that married women are more conservative than divorced or single women regarding attitudes toward feminism, and less likely to demonstrate a strong gender identification (see Klein, 1985; Rinehart, 1992).[14] Kopinak, on the other hand, found that marital status had no effect on the formation of political ideology (1987, 34). In Table 14, the impact of marital status on perceptions toward the issues of gender, mobility, and inequality is examined. It was found that divorced or separated women and widowed women are more likely to agree that gender is central to mobility, although the gap between their perceptions and those of married and single women does not go beyond 10%. It was further established that divorced or separated women show less support for education, hard work, and natural ability and considerably more support for personal ambition as factors crucial to mobility. One must be careful regarding conclusions here about the impact of being single on perceptions of inequality, since there could be interaction with the variable of age. In other words, we know from earlier discussion (see Table 12) that younger women were less likely to attach much significance to gender in opportunities for mobility; therefore we would expect that older single women may hold different attitudes than younger single women.

TABLE 14: WOMEN'S PERCEPTIONS OF MOBILITY AND FEMALE
INEQUALITY, BY MARITAL STATUS, IN PERCENTAGES

	Married or Common Law N=309	Widowed N=47	Divorced or Separated N=78	Single N=129
Women Suffer Very Serious Inequality	30.7	32.4	48.0	33.0
Women Deserve Top Priority in Action	28.5	34.3	48.0	31.1
Gender Is Essential or Very Important to Mobility	15.5	24.7	22.0	14.7

Nevertheless, the slightly stronger perception of the importance of gender among widowed women and divorced or separated women is of interest, because it suggests that women who are forced to take on new roles in the absence of male partners may acquire a stronger awareness of the significance of their gender. It must also be considered that women in these groups, particularly those with children still at home, are more likely to have a low income or to be unemployed. Statistics Canada, for example, reported that in 1992 the unemployment rate of female lone parents was 19.8% compared to 9.1% for women in two-parent families, and that 40% of female-headed lone parent families were low income families (Statistics Canada, 1992, 47-48). As a result, their experience of disparities in income or opportunity may yield a heightened awareness of, or sensitivity toward, the significance of gender to inequality.

In Table 14 we see this pattern appearing most clearly for women who are divorced or separated. They demonstrate almost a 20% higher level of support than women who are married or in a common law relationship for the belief that women suffer from very serious inequality *and* that they deserve top priority in action to redress that inequality, indicating a notable difference in the degree to which divorced or separated women voice dissatisfaction with the treatment of women and a sense of urgency to deal with the situation. Again, this is not surprising when we consider their increased probability of experiencing disparity relative to other women; there is likely to be a heightened sense of serious inequality and

TABLE 15: WOMEN'S PERCEPTIONS OF MOBILITY AND FEMALE INEQUALITY, BY LANGUAGE, IN PERCENTAGES

	English N=383	French N=125
Women Suffer Very Serious Inequality	27.7	45.3
Women Deserve Top Priority in Action	27.8	40.0
Gender Is Essential or Very Important to Mobility	20.2	4.6

an increased sense of urgency given their own economic situation. The fact that this "militancy" is not found to the same degree among women who are widowed may be related to the age of the women, rather than to their marital status. We have already found (see Table 10) that women over the age of 65, which is where the large majority of widows would be included, are the least likely of all age cohorts to see women's inequality as very serious or in need of immediate action.

Finally, we were interested in whether there were any large differences between the two official language communities when it came to the question of gendered inequality. Do women who claim English as their first language think differently about gender, mobility, and inequality than Francophone women? Based on the evidence presented in Table 15, there is reason to believe that cultural differences associated with language of origin do interact with gender in the formation of attitudes about gender, mobility, and inequality. We see that Francophone women are far less likely to accord much significance to the role of gender in mobility than Anglophone women; indeed, they demonstrate the lowest level of support for this factor among all the demographic groupings we have considered above. When we take all thirteen mobility-contributing factors into consideration, gender received the seventh highest level of support among Anglophone women, whereas it was eleventh among Francophone women. The latter are also much less inclined to identify hard work or natural ability as crucial to success than Anglophone women are. The implication then is that very few Francophone women believe one's opportunities are structured or significantly affected by one's gender. Yet, when they are asked directly about women's inequality, they are far more critical. As we see in Table 15, almost half of Francophone women believe that women suffer from very serious inequality, over a 17% difference from the percentage of Anglophone women who share this view. This is also combined with a stronger support for the priority of women's needs in social action programs, with approximately 13% more Francophone than Anglophone women perceiving that top priority should go to women over other groups or regions. We therefore have the curious situation where less than 5% of Francophone women believe gender plays a role in life's opportunities, yet 40% of this same group believe women are the group most urgently in need of intervention to reduce their inequality. This incongruity reflects perhaps the tenacity of meritocratic beliefs as they pertain to gender; it assumes that women are equal to men in opportunity but unequal in outcome. While we see this incongruity present among other groups of women, it appears most marked among Francophone women.

What do these patterns described above tell us about the consciousness of gender and its role in inequality among Canadian women? First, it appears that women do not uniformly speak with a "different voice" when they speak about gender and inequality. Indeed, the differences among women are frequently greater than the differences between men and women. Gender is not a pre-given identity that occupies a primary position in the formation of attitudes; rather, gender *interacts* with a series of other variables, and the form of that interaction is dependent on the salience of the issue at hand. Women's inequality, for example, appears to have a stronger salience among divorced or separated women. This salience is understandable if we examine the economic situation many of these women face; they have a stronger probability of experiencing economic inequality and a vested interest in seeing change occur. They also do not have the same structural barrier that married women have that might prevent them from seeing gender as a factor in mobility or seeing women's inequality as a very serious problem. Patricia Gurin describes this barrier as a consequence of women living with members of the "outgroup" (i.e., men). "Solidarity and recognition of group deprivation are fostered when category members interact most frequently with each other and only moderately with the outgroup" (1985, 145). Not only does the intimacy of the marital relation inhibit a recognition of group deprivation, but also, any successes and failures in social mobility are seen to accrue to the marital unit rather than to the individual.

Second, the analysis reveals the degree to which women in Canada continue to subscribe to an ideology of equal opportunity regarding gender, despite the evidence at hand that systemic gender inequality persists. Despite the variations between different demographic groups of women, the fact of the matter is that it is always a minority of women who believe that one's gender is very significant in affecting one's opportunities in life. This was true as well in terms of a cross-national pattern; other than in the Philippines, only a minority consider gender a key factor. The one exception to this pattern in Canada was within the small educational elite of women who have attended graduate school; here we found more scepticism for equal opportunity arguments and a much higher consciousness of gender as a key ingredient in social mobility.

Third, women are more likely to perceive an inequality of reward than of opportunity when it comes to gender. In every demographic grouping we find that its members are more likely to acknowledge that women suffer from very serious inequality than to concede that gender is an important explanatory factor for equality or inequality. Again, there are notable variations between the groups in the degree to which they believe this, but it is significant that women of all groups are more willing to recognize the existence of women's inequality than they are to recognize it as a structural feature of the way social mobility is organized.

Finally, we cannot say with any certainty that one demographic variable is a better predictor of women's attitudes than another. We know for example that age is correlated with a higher consciousness of gender's role in inequality for women between the ages of 45 and 54; but we need to take account of the historical context that underlies the formation of attitudes for this age group. In other words, more analysis would be needed to take account of the role of the women's movement in the '60s and '70s and the impact it may have had on the perceptions of this group at that stage in their life cycle. In a different context, we know that women employed part-time are less likely than women employed full-time to see gender as important to mobility or to say that women suffer from very serious inequality; nevertheless, they are more likely to claim the needs of women as a top priority for action. In other words, consciousness of gender and gender deprivation is not a simple consequence of any particular set of demographic variables; it is the result of an ongoing, dynamic process in which attitudes can shift within the same demographic category depending on the nature of the question.

In this discussion, the focus of the analysis has been on the question of whether there is a gendered nature to the way we think about inequality in Canada. In the first place, we were interested in whether men and women think differently about social inequality in general, and more specifically about gender inequality. Underlying this was an attempt to measure the presence of a "gender consciousness" about inequality, to determine whether women see themselves as unequal in this society.

We have found that there are more similarities than differences in the way men and women think about social inequality and its causes or justifications. For this reason we cannot say that men and women inhabit two distinct and differentiated worlds of perceptions regarding inequality. On important issues, such as locating the blame for social inequality at individual or social levels, or where they see manifest social conflict, we found the gender gap to be very small.

Men and women did differ notably in two general areas: in their views about the transformation of inequality, specifically in relation to the responsibility of government to do something, and in their views about the significance and gravity of women's inequality. On the question of women's stronger support for government intervention to redress inequality, it is difficult to determine from the data at hand whether or not it is the consequence of a more compassionate orientation among women. It could have more to do with the particular nature of women's relation to the welfare state. As Andrew (1984), Deitch (1988), and Erie and Rein (1988) have each pointed out, women have a different relation to the welfare state both as clients and as employees, and a definite stake in the expansion of the welfare state. Therefore, an increased demand for the government to take particular initiatives, such as guaranteeing a basic income, may reflect women's recognition of their self-interest in having the state provide greater economic security.

As regards the lesser significance men attached to gender as a factor in mobility, and, more importantly, their lower support for the gravity of women's inequality, this does indicate a different consciousness of gender and its role in inequality. While men and women both strongly endorse meritocratic assumptions regarding opportunity and mobility, women are more likely to recognize the outcome of the mobility contest as being weighted against them. This in turn leads them to place greater emphasis on the need to redress this inequality. Indeed, one could see this as a possible source of tension between men and women when we compare women's higher support against men's lower support for prompt intervention on behalf of women. If there are policy ramifications to these cleavages in opinion, they will likely be found in social action strategies to reduce gender inequality.

The intrasex differences we found in the recognition of women's inequality and of gender as a factor in mobility point to the difficulty of explanations centred around gender identity. Women's understanding of inequality is not simply a gendered understanding; gender may be a key variable here but it is still mediated by a series of other factors. It is important to understand how gender interacts with particular life experiences (education, employment, marriage, and so on) in particular historical contexts (during periods of economic instability, for example, or during periods when the women's movement is highly organized) to give shape to particular understandings of inequality. This approach neither denies the significance of gender to attitude formation, nor elevates it to essentialist status.

The real question we are left with, perhaps, is the task facing feminism. In the face of persistent disparities in income, employment, and mobility, the question is how to encourage or stimulate the collective self-consciousness of women as a political category. The politicization of women's inequality as an object of state reform and transformation requires a higher degree of gender consciousness than is now apparent.

ENDNOTES

1. A word of explanation on the use of the terms sex and gender throughout this chapter is warranted here. As much as possible I have tried to conform to the conventional usage of the term sex to refer to the biological categories of male and female. Hence, we can say that the survey sample was divided along sex lines for purposes of collating the data. Gender, on the other hand, refers to the socially and culturally constructed categories of males and females. In the most simple sense one has a sex, but one acquires a gender. In doing so one is inserted into a set of social relations that inform both social practice and ways of thinking about the world. Our gender is both something we "do" (in the sense of particular social roles and behaviours) and something we "think" (in the sense of particular ways of perceiving the world around us).

2. See Rinehart (1992, 12-13) for a discussion of some of the problems with empirical work in this field.

3. Norris (1988), for example, notes the stronger support for the Progressive Conservatives among male voters in the Canadian federal elections of 1980 and 1984, citing a gap ranging from 8 to 11%.

4. In a detailed examination of sex differences in voter preferences in the U.S. presidential elections of 1972, 1976, and 1980, Ethel Klein (1984) demonstrates that differences regarding support for campaign issues began to surface in 1972 and increased in strength over the eight years, with men voters becoming more conservative than women voters.

5. Zillah Eisenstein argues that the gender gap is, in fact, a consequence of two realities: "the tendency for females to think 'like' women because they are the nurturers of society" and "the fact that women believe in their right to equality (of opportunity)" (1984, 156).

6. In her analysis of voter data from the 1988 presidential election, Rinehart (1992) demonstrates that the gender gap between men and women in support for George Bush was actually caused by less than a third of all women voters. These were women whom she identified as having a high degree of "gender consciousness" and strong egalitarian preferences.

7. Erie and Rein (1988), for example, argue that the gender gap in the U.S. 1980 and 1984 elections was fuelled by the retrenchment in federal social programs to which women had a vested relationship, either as workers or as clients.

8. In the United States between 1970 and 1980, the proportion of poor who were female had increased from 1 out of 3 to 2 out of 3, according to Cynthia Deitch (1988, 196). In Canada, in 1992, 40% of female-headed, single-parent families with one income earner were classified as low income families (Statistics Canada, 1994, 48).

9. Statistics Canada notes that in 1991-92, women constituted 55% of the bachelor's level programs, 48% of master's level programs, and 36% of those in doctoral programs. In regard to their proportion of teaching faculty at the university level, they constitute only 21% (Statistics Canada, 1994, 37-38).

10. In the ISSP survey, only the first question appears on the internationally distributed survey; the second and third questions referred to in the above discussion were included in the Canadian version of the survey. In this section of the chapter, I am using only the data from the Canadian sample, which was composed of 1036 respondents, 495 males and 541 females.

11. See, for example, P. Gurin, who notes that "American polls taken since the early 1960s have always shown that men are somewhat more supportive than women of role equality" (1985, 152).

12. The remaining responses were divided between those who neither agreed nor disagreed and those who could not choose.

13. In fact, women with the lowest levels of education showed the highest levels of support among all age cohorts for more class-related explanations of mobility, such as "knowing the right people" (46.3%), "coming from a wealthy family" (15%), and "having political connections" (20%).

14. Interestingly, Klein found that men's marital status had no relation at all to their support for feminist views; rather, age was the determining factor (1985, 106).

REFERENCES

Andrew, Caroline. (1984). Women and the Welfare State. *Canadian Journal of Political Science, 17* (4), 667-83.

Barrett, Michele, & Anne Phillips. (1992). *Destabilizing Theory: Contemporary Feminist Debates.* Stanford: Stanford University Press.

Connell, R.W. (1987). *Gender and Power.* Stanford: Stanford University Press.

Deitch, Cynthia. (1988). Sex Differences in Support for Government Spending. In Mueller (1988), 192-216.

Eisenstein, Zillah. (1984). *Feminism and Sexual Equality.* New York: Monthly Review Press.

Erie, Steven, & Martin Rein. (1988). Women and the Welfare State. In Mueller (1988), 173-91.

Gilligan, Carol. (1982). *In a Different Voice.* Cambridge: Harvard University Press.

Gurin, Patricia. (1985). Women's Gender Consciousness. *Public Opinion Quarterly, 49,* 143-63.

Klein, Ethel. (1984). *Gender Politics.* Cambridge: Harvard University Press.

———. (1985). The Gender Gap: Different Issues, Different Answers. *The Brookings Review, 3* (2), 33-37.

Kopinak, Kathryn. (1987). Gender Differences in Political Ideology in Canada. *Canadian Review of Sociology and Anthropology, 24* (1), 23-38.

McCormack, Thelma. (1991). *Politics and the Hidden Injuries Of Gender.* Ottawa: CRIAW/ICREF.

Mueller, Carol M. (Ed.). (1988). *The Politics of the Gender Gap.* London: Sage.

Norris, Pippa. (1988). The Gender Gap: A Cross-National Trend. In Mueller (1988), 217-34.

Rinehart, Sue T. (1992). *Gender Consciousness and Politics.* London: Routledge.

Ruddick, Sara. (1980). Maternal Thinking, *Feminist Studies, 6* (2), 342-67.

Shapiro, Robert, & Harpreet Mahajan. (1986). Gender Differences in Policy Preferences: A Summary of Trends from the 1960s to the 1980s. *Public Opinion Quarterly, 50,* 42-61.

Smith, Tom. (1989). Inequality and Welfare. In R. Jowell, S. Witherspoon, & L. Brook (Eds.), *British Social Attitudes: Special International Report* (59-86). Brookfield VT: Gower.

Statistics Canada. (1994). *Women in the Labour Force: 1994 Edition.* Ottawa.

RESPONSES TO SELECTED QUESTIONS FROM THE 1992 ISSP SURVEY
ON SOCIAL INEQUALITY

Question 1
Importance for Getting Ahead in Life:
a) Coming from a wealthy family

Importance:	Essential	Very	Fairly	Not very	Not at all	# of Cases
Australia	6%	19	29	37	11	2131
West Germany	6%	14	28	35	17	2220
East Germany	8%	15	26	32	19	1054
Great Britain	3%	13	32	33	19	1053
United States	3%	15	32	32	18	1230
Austria	11%	21	30	23	15	998
Hungary	12%	18	38	24	8	1232
Italy	7%	29	32	20	13	995
Norway	2%	9	36	39	15	1515
Sweden	3%	13	37	34	13	701
Czech Rep.	9%	10	25	43	13	1076
Slovenia	4%	18	31	26	22	1024
Poland	15%	40	27	9	9	1528
Bulgaria	26%	16	29	22	7	1105
Russia	19%	22	27	19	13	1774
New Zealand	2%	12	36	33	17	1216
Canada	3%	11	30	35	22	987
Philippines	10%	32	25	30	4	1196

b) Having well-educated parents

Importance:	Essential	Very	Fairly	Not very	Not at all	# of Cases
Australia	6%	24	39	25	7	2133
West Germany	6%	26	43	18	7	2255
East Germany	6%	28	39	20	7	1073
Great Britain	4%	24	46	19	6	1057
United States	6%	36	41	13	4	1246
Austria	9%	27	34	21	9	1005
Hungary	6%	14	38	34	8	1229
Italy	6%	37	36	15	6	993
Norway	1%	10	40	36	12	1516
Sweden	3%	21	44	23	9	705
Czech Rep.	5%	7	21	49	18	1076
Slovenia	3%	24	36	23	14	1025
Poland	9%	36	33	12	10	1566
Bulgaria	15%	20	36	23	6	1071
Russia	12%	21	27	27	13	1843
New Zealand	5%	27	48	16	4	1223
Canada	4%	24	49	17	6	992
Philippines	19%	56	17	7	1	1199

c) Having a good education yourself

Importance:	Essential	Very	Fairly	Not very	Not at all	# of Cases
Australia	25%	47	26	2	1	2135
West Germany	34%	55	10	2	1	2279
East Germany	36%	55	8	1	—	1083
Great Britain	24%	50	23	2	1	1062
United States	35%	52	12	1	—	1255
Austria	46%	46	7	1	—	1017
Hungary	10%	19	46	21	5	1224
Italy	28%	53	17	2	1	994
Norway	13%	48	33	5	1	1521
Sweden	12%	57	28	2	1	728
Czech Rep.	14%	16	32	30	8	1081
Slovenia	18%	45	28	6	2	1031
Poland	14%	50	27	7	3	1596
Bulgaria	29%	29	29	10	2	1122
Russia	20%	31	25	18	5	1879
New Zealand	33%	45	21	2	—	1230
Canada	35%	50	15	1	—	998
Philippines	32%	58	8	2	—	1200

d) Ambition

Importance:	Essential	Very	Fairly	Not very	Not at all	# of Cases
Australia	36%	45	18	1	—	2143
West Germany	17%	46	30	6	2	2271
East Germany	23%	53	18	5	1	1083
Great Britain	33%	42	22	3	1	1058
United States	39%	51	9	1	—	1251
Austria	39%	44	14	2	1	1016
Hungary	19%	36	38	6	1	1223
Italy	22%	36	26	12	5	989
Norway	38%	44	16	1	—	1513
Sweden	23%	59	17	1	1	717
Czech Rep.	26%	30	33	9	3	1077
Slovenia	24%	42	24	7	3	1000
Poland	24%	58	14	3	2	1578
Bulgaria	42%	30	23	5	1	1078
Russia	14%	27	32	18	9	1650
New Zealand	42%	42	15	1	—	1230
Canada	42%	42	14	2	—	999
Philippines	29%	58	9	3	1	1200

e) Natural ability

Importance:	Essential	Very	Fairly	Not very	Not at all	# of Cases
Australia	18%	48	31	3	—	2139
West Germany	14%	39	36	9	2	2247
East Germany	9%	38	38	12	3	1071
Great Britain	12%	43	40	4	1	1054
United States	10%	43	42	6	—	1233
Austria	28%	43	25	4	1	1010
Hungary	21%	30	41	7	1	1216
Italy	23%	49	23	5	1	991
Norway	11%	39	43	7	1	1505
Sweden	8%	38	47	6	1	713
Czech Rep.	24%	32	33	9	2	1085
Slovenia	16%	43	32	7	3	1019
Poland	30%	57	11	2	1	1605
Bulgaria	30%	27	30	11	2	1061
Russia	32%	40	21	5	2	1847
New Zealand	13%	38	41	8	—	1227
Canada	9%	36	46	7	2	985
Philippines	26%	58	13	3	1	1198

f) Hard work

Importance:	Essential	Very	Fairly	Not very	Not at all	# of Cases
Australia	33%	48	18	2	—	2143
West Germany	14%	38	36	10	2	2257
East Germany	20%	51	23	5	1	1074
Great Britain	34%	50	14	2	—	1061
United States	38%	50	11	1	—	1266
Austria	27%	40	25	7	1	1014
Hungary	20%	34	33	11	2	1228
Italy	16%	38	30	12	3	986
Norway	24%	48	23	4	1	1510
Sweden	17%	51	27	4	2	725
Czech Rep.	33%	38	24	4	1	1094
Slovenia	17%	36	26	16	5	1036
Poland	26%	56	14	3	2	1611
Bulgaria	42%	29	22	6	1	1105
Russia	27%	32	23	13	6	1874
New Zealand	42%	42	14	2	—	1226
Canada	36%	44	17	3	—	994
Philippines	34%	54	10	2	—	1200

g) Knowing the right people

Importance:	Essential	Very	Fairly	Not very	Not at all	# of Cases
Australia	15%	28	39	15	3	2127
West Germany	15%	38	33	12	2	2256
East Germany	21%	38	28	11	3	1065
Great Britain	11%	24	45	18	3	1059
United States	9%	34	42	13	2	1252
Austria	27%	37	28	6	2	1012
Hungary	13%	26	38	19	3	1214
Italy	23%	50	21	5	2	994
Norway	9%	22	42	24	3	1504
Sweden	8%	31	41	17	4	707
Czech Rep.	20%	31	37	10	2	1083
Slovenia	14%	41	33	9	4	1022
Poland	17%	45	30	6	3	1577
Bulgaria	22%	24	33	17	4	1059
Russia	31%	31	28	7	4	1888
New Zealand	9%	21	46	20	4	1225
Canada	11%	24	49	15	2	992
Philippines	14%	45	25	14	2	1197

h) Having political connections

Importance:	Essential	Very	Fairly	Not very	Not at all	# of Cases
Australia	7%	14	24	44	11	2120
West Germany	5%	13	26	37	18	2187
East Germany	4%	13	23	39	22	1022
Great Britain	2%	5	15	47	30	1022
United States	4%	15	29	38	15	1223
Austria	18%	22	29	23	9	988
Hungary	7%	15	32	35	12	1176
Italy	19%	32	23	15	12	981
Norway	3%	7	19	47	25	1444
Sweden	3%	8	18	45	27	670
Czech Rep.	5%	10	22	44	21	1041
Slovenia	5%	18	24	28	25	966
Poland	6%	20	31	24	19	1397
Bulgaria	14%	11	17	33	25	959
Russia	10%	10	17	33	30	1405
New Zealand	2%	3	10	41	44	1208
Canada	4%	9	27	40	21	970
Philippines	9%	25	28	32	7	1195

i) A person's race

Importance:	Essential	Very	Fairly	Not very	Not at all	# of Cases
Australia	5%	16	29	38	12	2119
West Germany	7%	14	19	27	32	2175
East Germany	5%	13	18	29	35	1023
Great Britain	2%	14	32	30	22	1014
United States	3%	13	25	33	26	1222
Austria	9%	13	20	26	33	947
Hungary	4%	8	29	39	21	1197
Italy	3%	12	17	24	45	966
Norway	3%	15	34	34	15	1411
Sweden	3%	8	23	31	35	665
Czech Rep.	2%	3	10	40	45	1059
Slovenia	2%	8	13	25	51	957
Poland	2%	7	16	24	50	1355
Bulgaria	3%	4	12	33	48	960
Russia	2%	4	10	32	52	1702
New Zealand	2%	9	20	34	35	1207
Canada	3%	8	23	34	32	978
Philippines	10%	43	26	18	3	1195

j) A person's religion

Importance:	Essential	Very	Fairly	Not very	Not at all	# of Cases
Australia	1%	3	11	59	25	2117
West Germany	2%	6	12	33	47	2212
East Germany	1%	4	7	30	58	1036
Great Britain	2%	2	10	42	46	1039
United States	5%	10	15	34	37	1248
Austria	2%	5	11	33	49	980
Hungary	2%	3	11	37	48	1220
Italy	3%	12	13	30	42	969
Norway	2%	4	11	42	41	1444
Sweden	1%	3	8	35	54	652
Czech Rep.	2%	2	5	33	58	1064
Slovenia	2%	7	15	26	51	1007
Poland	4%	15	19	20	42	1484
Bulgaria	4%	3	10	28	55	995
Russia	2%	3	6	27	63	1666
New Zealand	3%	3	6	28	60	1218
Canada	3%	3	7	33	55	985
Philippines	13%	46	22	15	3	1199

k) The region of the country a person grew up in

Importance:	Essential	Very	Fairly	Not very	Not at all	# of Cases
Australia	2%	7	20	52	19	2131
West Germany	1%	5	11	34	50	2198
East Germany	2%	5	9	34	50	1042
Great Britain	1%	4	20	42	33	1047
United States	1%	5	15	40	38	1239
Austria	1%	2	8	28	60	986
Hungary	2%	5	21	34	38	1199
Italy	1%	14	23	29	33	969
Norway	1%	4	18	40	37	1499
Sweden	1%	2	9	31	57	687
Czech Rep.	2%	5	17	40	36	1073
Slovenia	1%	5	14	24	56	996
Poland	2%	10	28	22	38	1560
Bulgaria	3%	5	18	30	44	1016
Russia	3%	10	25	51	11	1979
New Zealand	2%	5	16	33	44	1216
Canada	1%	7	24	31	36	987
Philippines	9%	42	27	18	4	1198

l) Being born a man or a woman

Importance:	Essential	Very	Fairly	Not very	Not at all	# of Cases
Australia	5%	12	24	42	17	2134
West Germany	4%	11	20	28	38	2157
East Germany	5%	11	17	28	40	1020
Great Britain	2%	11	25	33	29	1017
United States	3%	15	25	33	25	1217
Austria	4%	11	24	26	35	970
Hungary	2%	4	25	35	33	1216
Italy	1%	14	24	25	35	972
Norway	2%	5	20	43	30	1471
Sweden	3%	8	27	33	29	675
Czech Rep.	5%	5	17	38	36	1070
Slovenia	2%	9	24	26	39	1006
Poland	4%	15	29	18	34	1492
Bulgaria	6%	9	19	29	36	1019
Russia	3%	21	27	38	11	1982
New Zealand	3%	8	16	28	45	1183
Canada	4%	11	21	28	37	963
Philippines	12%	46	23	15	4	1199

m) A person's political beliefs

Importance:	Essential	Very	Fairly	Not very	Not at all	# of Cases
Australia	1%	4	13	57	25	2128
West Germany	2%	15	29	30	25	2186
East Germany	3%	15	28	33	21	1026
Great Britain	1%	6	22	42	29	1034
United States	2%	9	24	40	25	1219
Austria	4%	13	28	29	26	965
Hungary	5%	5	24	40	27	1171
Italy	2%	16	27	29	25	962
Norway	1%	4	19	44	32	1398
Sweden	2%	4	18	40	37	672
Czech Rep.	5%	8	26	38	23	1019
Slovenia	1%	9	24	26	40	930
Poland	3%	13	31	23	30	1392
Bulgaria	4%	5	17	29	46	966
Russia	3%	7	19	35	36	1469
New Zealand	1%	4	15	36	45	1201
Canada	1%	6	20	40	33	966
Philippines	6%	30	30	27	7	1193

Question 2
The way things are in [country] people like me and my family have a good chance of improving our standard of living.

	Strongly Agree	Agree	Neither	Disagree	Strongly Disagree	# of Cases
Australia	9%	40	30	18	3	2065
West Germany	3%	32	34	24	8	2031
East Germany	3%	36	26	25	10	991
Great Britain	4%	26	29	32	10	1033
United States	11%	44	20	20	5	1235
Austria	8%	45	28	15	5	958
Hungary	2%	9	24	37	28	1231
Italy	7%	35	24	24	9	972
Norway	3%	27	36	29	6	1450
Sweden	1%	21	46	24	8	693
Czech Rep.	7%	25	20	33	15	1062
Slovenia	2%	17	24	41	16	965
Poland	2%	10	15	43	30	1370
Bulgaria	6%	21	16	14	40	1024
Russia	6%	14	14	31	33	1525
New Zealand	4%	23	23	36	13	1206
Canada	6%	31	25	29	9	961
Philippines	12%	58	23	6	1	1198

Question 3
a) People would not want to take extra responsibility at work unless they were paid for it.

	Strongly Agree	Agree	Neither	Disagree	Strongly Disagree	# of Cases
Australia	16%	63	12	9	1	2137
West Germany	19%	53	9	16	2	2169
East Germany	16%	56	9	18	2	1025
Great Britain	20%	58	9	12	1	1056
United States	15%	51	11	20	3	1247
Austria	22%	49	11	15	4	995
Hungary	13%	50	18	16	3	1204
Italy	37%	48	7	7	1	993
Norway	10%	54	13	20	2	1503
Sweden	19%	58	13	9	1	730
Czech Rep.	14%	54	13	15	4	1066
Slovenia	20%	54	13	12	2	998
Poland	33%	50	7	8	2	1530
Bulgaria	69%	22	4	2	3	1098
Russia	66%	24	3	4	3	1911
New Zealand	16%	58	10	14	2	1219
Canada	15%	46	15	22	3	989
Philippines	7%	50	25	17	2	1199

b) Workers would not bother to get skills and qualifications unless they were paid extra for having them.

	Strongly Agree	Agree	Neither	Disagree	Strongly Disagree	# of Cases
Australia	14%	60	14	12	1	2133
West Germany	22%	56	8	13	2	2182
East Germany	16%	59	8	15	2	1046
Great Britain	17%	47	13	21	2	1051
United States	11%	44	12	30	3	1244
Austria	25%	54	10	9	2	996
Hungary	11%	49	21	16	3	1199
Italy	29%	51	9	9	2	987
Norway	7%	40	19	31	4	1500
Sweden	15%	55	17	12	2	724
Czech Rep.	15%	47	14	19	5	1076
Slovenia	14%	54	15	16	1	998
Poland	27%	51	9	12	2	1529
Bulgaria	66%	24	4	3	4	1085
Russia	48%	25	5	14	8	1851
New Zealand	16%	45	11	24	4	1219
Canada	9%	40	14	31	6	989
Philippines	8%	47	26	17	2	1197

c) Inequality continues because it benefits the rich and powerful.

	Strongly Agree	Agree	Neither	Disagree	Strongly Disagree	# of Cases
Australia	17%	42	24	15	2	2113
West Germany	27%	48	12	10	3	2118
East Germany	37%	49	7	5	2	1038
Great Britain	24%	41	18	16	2	1005
United States	18%	41	19	19	4	1211
Austria	26%	42	17	12	4	968
Hungary	17%	35	20	21	7	1191
Italy	30%	46	13	9	2	975
Norway	21%	52	15	11	2	1481
Sweden	21%	32	25	17	5	680
Czech Rep.	21%	39	16	18	6	1039
Slovenia	20%	54	12	12	3	954
Poland	29%	44	12	12	3	1438
Bulgaria	58%	21	11	4	6	1033
Russia	48%	30	7	10	6	1671
New Zealand	27%	35	15	19	5	1183
Canada	27%	35	19	15	4	973
Philippines	9%	42	23	22	4	1198

d) No one would study for years to become a lawyer or doctor unless they expected to earn a lot more than ordinary workers.

	Strongly Agree	Agree	Neither	Disagree	Strongly Disagree	# of Cases
Australia	31%	50	10	8	1	2133
West Germany	40%	48	5	6	1	2217
East Germany	34%	54	5	7	1	1047
Great Britain	23%	47	11	17	1	1054
United States	25%	45	10	18	2	1261
Austria	47%	40	6	6	2	997
Hungary	20%	40	20	16	4	1210
Italy	37%	36	11	12	4	990
Norway	16%	49	16	17	2	1503
Sweden	25%	47	14	12	2	721
Czech Rep.	23%	39	13	19	6	1071
Slovenia	22%	47	16	14	2	1015
Poland	33%	45	9	11	1	1508
Bulgaria	67%	21	4	4	6	1070
Russia	37%	28	7	18	9	1778
New Zealand	25%	48	10	15	3	1219
Canada	22%	40	12	21	5	987
Philippines	10%	52	24	12	1	1199

e) Large differences in income are necessary for [country's] prosperity.

	Strongly Agree	Agree	Neither	Disagree	Strongly Disagree	# of Cases
Australia	4%	21	32	34	9	2118
West Germany	4%	17	23	38	18	2092
East Germany	2%	11	14	47	26	1002
Great Britain	4%	15	22	46	13	1033
United States	4%	22	23	38	13	1222
Austria	4%	13	22	33	28	964
Hungary	3%	18	18	40	21	1172
Italy	6%	26	23	26	18	958
Norway	2%	15	20	48	15	1448
Sweden	5%	25	31	30	9	673
Czech Rep.	8%	20	19	40	13	995
Slovenia	5%	25	20	41	10	965
Poland	9%	26	17	38	10	1397
Bulgaria	15%	13	14	12	46	935
Russia	14%	20	12	24	31	1424
New Zealand	2%	15	20	46	17	1187
Canada	3%	13	18	45	21	967
Philippines	10%	49	27	12	2	1197

f) Allowing business to make good profits is the best way to improve everyone's standard of living.

	Strongly Agree	Agree	Neither	Disagree	Strongly Disagree	# of Cases
Australia	8%	42	27	19	3	2119
West Germany	6%	35	22	27	10	2008
East Germany	5%	36	15	31	13	973
Great Britain	8%	37	19	30	6	1030
United States	8%	41	20	26	7	1228
Austria	9%	32	27	22	10	918
Hungary	10%	37	26	20	7	1153
Italy	13%	50	15	14	7	969
Norway	7%	34	27	26	6	1362
Sweden	9%	36	29	22	4	640
Czech Rep.	13%	40	19	21	7	1031
Slovenia	11%	48	18	20	3	939
Poland	20%	51	15	12	3	1336
Bulgaria	32%	23	15	10	20	928
Russia	18%	27	10	22	24	1543
New Zealand	8%	38	21	27	6	1200
Canada	3%	31	25	29	8	963
Philippines	7%	40	27	22	4	1197

g) Inequality continues to exist because ordinary people don't join together to get rid of it.

	Strongly Agree	Agree	Neither	Disagree	Strongly Disagree	# of Cases
Australia	4%	25	36	30	5	2100
West Germany	13%	34	21	25	7	2011
East Germany	13%	41	17	24	5	958
Great Britain	7%	34	25	29	5	1010
United States	11%	39	20	27	4	1218
Austria	15%	36	22	21	7	934
Hungary	7%	28	22	30	14	1177
Italy	20%	47	15	12	6	976
Norway	7%	39	24	25	6	1415
Sweden	8%	27	29	28	7	632
Czech Rep.	14%	38	17	22	9	1027
Slovenia	9%	42	19	27	3	904
Poland	14%	42	19	20	4	1280
Bulgaria	39%	19	15	9	18	863
Russia	25%	23	11	21	21	1472
New Zealand	8%	38	22	33	7	1179
Canada	11%	36	21	25	7	968
Philippines	6%	44	31	16	3	1194

Question 6
a) Differences in income in [country] are too large.

	Strongly Agree	Agree	Neither	Disagree	Strongly Disagree	# of Cases
Australia	18%	45	19	15	2	2085
West Germany	31%	53	9	6	1	2173
East Germany	61%	37	1	1	—	1061
Great Britain	36%	45	11	7	1	1039
United States	28%	49	11	10	2	1244
Austria	35%	47	10	6	1	998
Hungary	45%	39	8	6	2	1227
Italy	53%	36	6	4	—	993
Norway	22%	49	14	12	3	1512
Sweden	24%	35	22	14	5	726
Czech Rep.	36%	47	6	9	2	1083
Slovenia	48%	38	6	7	1	1031
Poland	42%	44	6	8	1	1539
Bulgaria	85%	12	2	1	1	1127
Russia	58%	30	4	4	3	1784
New Zealand	30%	43	14	12	2	1192
Canada	25%	45	16	11	2	980
Philippines	9%	50	23	17	1	1193

b) It is the responsibility of the government to reduce the differences in income between people with high incomes and those with low incomes.

	Strongly Agree	Agree	Neither	Disagree	Strongly Disagree	# of Cases
Australia	10%	33	20	29	8	2091
West Germany	20%	46	15	15	5	2130
East Germany	42%	47	5	6	—	1051
Great Britain	26%	39	14	17	4	1025
United States	10%	29	20	29	13	1216
Austria	28%	42	13	14	4	988
Hungary	33%	42	14	9	3	1233
Italy	40%	40	10	8	2	991
Norway	17%	43	16	18	6	1472
Sweden	17%	36	18	19	10	714
Czech Rep.	24%	44	11	18	4	1070
Slovenia	31%	49	9	10	1	1009
Poland	31%	47	10	11	3	1531
Bulgaria	61%	21	8	3	8	1073
Russia	36%	29	10	17	9	1715
New Zealand	16%	37	16	23	8	1186
Canada	16%	32	21	21	10	964
Philippines	10%	47	27	16	1	1193

c) The government should provide a job for everyone who wants one.

	Strongly Agree	Agree	Neither	Disagree	Strongly Disagree	# of Cases
Australia	10%	30	22	32	7	2091
West Germany	22%	44	15	14	5	2177
East Germany	55%	37	4	3	—	1072
Great Britain	22%	34	17	22	5	1030
United States	16%	31	14	29	10	1242
Austria	31%	41	14	10	4	995
Hungary	51%	34	9	5	1	1242
Italy	57%	30	8	5	1	993
Norway	37%	41	13	8	1	1511
Sweden	27%	45	17	8	2	725
Czech Rep.	36%	42	7	11	4	1088
Slovenia	36%	45	10	9	1	1025
Poland	49%	40	5	5	1	1593
Bulgaria	70%	16	7	3	5	1113
Russia	73%	21	2	2	1	1928
New Zealand	19%	30	18	27	5	1181
Canada	16%	24	19	31	11	971
Philippines	29%	57	12	2	—	1198

d) The government should provide everyone with a guaranteed basic income.

	Strongly Agree	Agree	Neither	Disagree	Strongly Disagree	# of Cases
Australia	10%	40	19	25	6	2086
West Germany	22%	39	14	20	9	2127
East Germany	51%	37	5	6	1	1050
Great Britain	27%	39	10	20	4	1039
United States	10%	24	15	33	18	1228
Austria	14%	37	17	20	12	952
Hungary	50%	35	10	5	1	1239
Italy	36%	33	10	14	7	989
Norway	35%	43	9	10	2	1504
Sweden	10%	33	25	21	11	691
Czech Rep.	30%	36	11	18	5	1077
Slovenia	27%	51	11	11	1	1015
Poland	47%	40	6	7	1	1576
Bulgaria	77%	13	5	3	3	1125
Russia	69%	23	3	3	2	1902
New Zealand	21%	40	13	22	5	1185
Canada	18%	30	13	27	11	976
Philippines	28%	56	13	2	—	1196

Question 7
Generally, how would you describe taxes in [country] today. (We mean all taxes together, including [national insurance/social security], income tax, [GST/sales tax] and all the rest.)
a) For those with high incomes, are taxes ...

	Much too high	Too high	About right	Too low	Much too low	# of Cases
Australia	5%	22	31	34	7	2054
West Germany	2%	7	27	48	17	2107
East Germany	1%	3	16	47	33	985
Great Britain	4%	14	37	36	9	1030
United States	8%	10	17	40	26	1180
Austria	3%	12	31	41	14	911
Hungary	8%	18	31	33	11	1059
Italy	10%	19	—	39	32	958
Norway	8%	18	27	34	12	1463
Sweden	8%	17	30	33	12	667
Czech Rep.	7%	16	28	36	13	953
Slovenia	3%	11	39	39	7	774
Poland	6%	15	32	34	13	1285
Bulgaria	5%	15	24	41	15	903
Russia	16%	27	42	10	6	1300
New Zealand	6%	12	28	43	12	1166
Canada	10%	15	18	37	20	948
Philippines	14%	34	42	8	1	1185

b) Now, for those with middle incomes, are taxes ...

	Much too high	Too high	About right	Too low	Much too low	# of Cases
Australia	5%	22	31	34	7	2054
Australia	7%	47	42	3	—	2069
West Germany	4%	42	50	3	—	2166
East Germany	3%	28	60	9	—	987
Great Britain	5%	33	56	6	—	1029
United States	25%	53	20	2	—	1216
Austria	6%	43	50	2	—	934
Hungary	17%	53	27	3	—	1109
Italy	23%	67	—	9	1	967
Norway	11%	44	43	2	—	1487
Sweden	12%	43	44	1	—	673
Czech Rep.	8%	47	41	4	—	1039
Slovenia	5%	42	49	4	1	785
Poland	10%	44	42	4	1	1314
Bulgaria	10%	55	31	4	—	956
Russia	19%	40	39	1	—	1452
New Zealand	10%	41	46	3	—	1192
Canada	32%	48	18	2	—	977
Philippines	4%	25	56	13	1	1186

c) Lastly, for those with low incomes, are taxes ...

	Much too high	Too high	About right	Too low	Much too low	# of Cases
Australia	19%	50	30	1	—	2068
West Germany	36%	50	13	1	—	2169
East Germany	44%	50	7	—	—	1026
Great Britain	31%	51	17	1	—	1037
United States	31%	44	23	1	1	1190
Austria	32%	47	21	—	—	946
Hungary	48%	38	12	1	—	1142
Italy	68%	31	—	1	1	977
Norway	37%	48	15	1	—	1480
Sweden	36%	48	16	—	—	686
Czech Rep.	35%	45	18	1	1	1052
Slovenia	45%	46	8	—	—	822
Poland	42%	43	14	1	—	1406
Bulgaria	54%	34	10	1	—	1000
Russia	35%	30	32	2	2	1389
New Zealand	27%	46	26	1	—	1186
Canada	40%	38	20	2	1	956
Philippines	9%	20	33	25	14	1179

Question 8
Do you think that people with high incomes should pay a larger share of their income in taxes than those with low incomes, the same share, or a smaller share?

	Much larger	Larger	Same share	Smaller	Much smaller	# of Cases
Australia	17%	54	27	1	—	2059
West Germany	30%	58	12	1	—	2120
East Germany	44%	50	5	—	—	1042
United States	27%	47	24	1	1	1204
Austria	26%	57	17	1	—	945
Hungary	23%	58	15	3	1	1118
Italy	40%	46	13	1	—	987
Norway	13%	60	23	2	1	1452
Sweden	14%	62	23	1	—	717
Czech Rep.	28%	58	13	—	—	1060
Slovenia	25%	61	13	1	—	967
Poland	23%	53	18	5	1	1413
Bulgaria	69%	26	4	1	1	988
Russia	20%	45	24	9	2	1450
New Zealand	13%	60	27	1	—	1193
Canada	23%	51	25	1	—	976
Philippines	29%	34	29	6	2	1181

Question 9
In all countries there are differences or even conflicts between different social groups. In your opinion, in [country], how much conflict is there between ...
a) Poor people and rich people

	Very strong	Strong	Not very strong	None	# of Cases
Australia	5%	30	58	6	2090
West Germany	9%	30	51	10	2052
East Germany	17%	46	34	3	991
Great Britain	14%	46	38	2	1017
United States	21%	48	28	3	1198
Austria	6%	25	51	18	946
Hungary	27%	44	26	3	1222
Italy	21%	36	31	11	978
Norway	4%	15	68	14	1443
Sweden	6%	24	63	7	702
Czech Rep.	7%	25	51	17	913
Slovenia	11%	32	40	17	944
Poland	15%	41	34	10	1388
Bulgaria	19%	36	26	19	1005
Russia	21%	41	29	8	1754
New Zealand	12%	43	41	4	1189
Canada	14%	33	46	7	966
Philippines	18%	37	34	11	1198

b) The working class and the middle class

	Very strong	Strong	Not very strong	None	# of Cases
Australia	1%	12	73	15	2093
West Germany	2%	11	59	29	2083
East Germany	2%	15	64	19	967
Great Britain	4%	22	65	9	1013
United States	5%	24	59	13	1183
Austria	1%	10	53	36	929
Hungary	5%	24	56	15	1202
Italy	11%	33	41	15	971
Norway	1%	4	62	33	1422
Sweden	1%	8	71	21	705
Czech Rep.	2%	11	57	31	988
Slovenia	2%	19	53	26	960
Poland	6%	28	50	16	1391
Bulgaria	2%	15	39	44	959
Russia	6%	16	48	31	1789
New Zealand	2%	11	68	19	1170
Canada	2%	12	65	20	954
Philippines	7%	29	49	15	1194

c) The unemployed and people with jobs

	Very strong	Strong	Not very strong	None	# of Cases
Australia	5%	31	55	9	2082
West Germany	7%	34	45	14	2074
East Germany	11%	39	39	11	1005
Great Britain	11%	35	45	9	1008
United States	12%	40	39	8	1178
Austria	7%	36	40	17	934
Hungary	14%	35	38	15	1204
Italy	19%	36	27	18	976
Norway	5%	20	56	20	1408
Sweden	2%	14	63	21	671
Czech Rep.	6%	20	43	32	914
Slovenia	8%	31	36	25	955
Poland	9%	28	39	24	1357
Bulgaria	10%	26	34	30	991
Russia	5%	16	35	44	1493
New Zealand	11%	39	41	9	1169
Canada	8%	29	48	15	962
Philippines	10%	33	43	15	1196

d) Management and workers

	Very strong	Strong	Not very strong	None	# of Cases
Australia	5%	39	54	2	2085
West Germany	10%	40	44	7	2068
East Germany	18%	53	27	2	987
Great Britain	8%	43	46	3	1015
United States	14%	51	32	2	1190
Austria	5%	33	49	13	934
Hungary	21%	43	32	5	1186
Italy	13%	37	38	12	968
Norway	2%	21	72	5	1415
Sweden	4%	24	62	10	681
Czech Rep.	9%	42	42	7	999
Slovenia	20%	54	21	5	992
Poland	8%	37	47	8	1366
Bulgaria	13%	40	32	15	993
Russia	14%	34	39	13	1764
New Zealand	10%	40	46	4	1177
Canada	15%	46	38	2	963
Philippines	15%	38	38	10	1188

e) Farmers and city people

	Very strong	Strong	Not very strong	None	# of Cases
Australia	5%	34	52	9	2082
West Germany	2%	9	49	41	2047
East Germany	2%	12	49	38	972
Great Britain	7%	27	51	16	986
United States	11%	25	48	16	1153
Austria	3%	15	45	37	942
Hungary	7%	23	48	23	1202
Italy	5%	18	32	45	956
Norway	5%	24	56	16	1423
Sweden	2%	13	61	25	677
Czech Rep.	1%	12	41	45	957
Slovenia	4%	25	39	32	960
Poland	7%	26	45	22	1406
Bulgaria	5%	16	31	49	983
Russia	5%	16	39	40	1752
New Zealand	5%	20	53	22	1178
Canada	6%	18	52	24	944
Philippines	10%	28	44	19	1190

f) Young people and older people

	Very strong	Strong	Not very strong	None	# of Cases
Australia	5%	34	52	9	2082
Australia	5%	28	58	9	2090
West Germany	5%	27	55	14	2120
East Germany	4%	24	56	15	1004
Great Britain	8%	31	49	13	1007
United States	11%	32	46	10	1195
Austria	7%	31	45	16	975
Hungary	7%	27	48	18	1220
Italy	7%	24	42	27	970
Norway	2%	14	65	20	1425
Sweden	2%	12	61	25	696
Czech Rep.	4%	18	54	24	999
Slovenia	5%	26	43	26	984
Poland	6%	27	49	17	1412
Bulgaria	10%	28	38	24	1016
Russia	6%	20	39	35	1779
New Zealand	5%	21	54	20	1183
Canada	6%	21	55	19	950
Philippines	9%	24	47	21	1189

CONTRIBUTORS

Scott Bennett is associate professor of Political Science at Carleton University. He is a consultant on, and a writer about, public opinion and public policy issues.

Carl J. Cuneo is professor of Sociology at McMaster University, Hamilton. He has published over 30 articles and book chapters on different aspects of inequality over the past 20 years. His *Pay Equity: The Labour-Feminist Challenge* was published by Oxford University Press in 1990.

Jeffrey Frank works for Statistics Canada in Ottawa. He is an editor of the quarterly publication *Canadian Social Trends.*

Leslie S. Laczko is an associate professor of Sociology at the University of Ottawa. He is the author of a number of articles on language and ethnicity in Canada, as well as the recently-published monograph *Pluralism and Inequality in Quebec.*

Eileen Saunders is an associate professor in the School of Journalism and Communication at Carleton University. She is the author of several journal articles on the role of women in Canadian society and communications.

The editors wish to thank **Heather Pyman** for her help in organizing the Canadian study.